The Hero Maker

Learn how to turn your school board members into heroes by helping them make smart, worthwhile decisions that they will deserve to brag about. In this much-needed book, Ryan Donlan and Todd Whitaker offer practical strategies to help superintendents develop better working relationships with their boards. You'll discover how to:

- ◆ reconnect board members to the real purpose of education, despite their agendas
- ◆ work with your board more effectively during meetings and at times in between
- ◆ guide board members into more productive roles when they overreach beyond policymaking
- ◆ connect and communicate with board members regardless of personality
- ◆ encourage board members to play to their strengths
- ◆ start each school year undefeated and know when it is time to move on.

Each chapter contains hero-making tips to help you get started. The book also includes a special feature on board personalities and the Process Communication Model® (PCM), a method that will make it easier to avoid miscommunication with board members. With this practical book, you'll be able to overcome the challenges of the superintendent–board relationship so that your board can make better decisions for those who matter most—the students.

Ryan Donlan is an Assistant Professor of Educational Leadership at Indiana State University and specializes in helping schools with leadership and governance. He has co-authored three books, including *Minds Unleashed: How Principals Can Lead the Right-Brained Way*.

Todd Whitaker is a Professor of Educational Leadership at the University of Missouri. He is a leading presenter in the field of education and has written more than 40 books, including the national best seller, *What Great Teachers Do Differently*.

The Hero Maker

How Superintendents Can Get Their School Boards to Do the Right Thing

Ryan Donlan and Todd Whitaker

Routledge
Taylor & Francis Group

NEW YORK AND LONDON

First published 2017
by Routledge
711 Third Avenue, New York, NY 10017

and by Routledge
2 Park Square, Milton Park, Abingdon, Oxon, OX14 4RN

Routledge is an imprint of the Taylor & Francis Group, an informa business

Library of Congress Cataloging-in-Publication Data
Names: Whitaker, Todd; Donlan, Ryan, authors.
Title: The hero maker : how superintendents can get their school
    boards to do the right thing / by Todd Whitaker and Ryan Donlan.
Description: New York : Routledge, [2017]
Identifiers: LCCN 2016036572| ISBN 9781138961173 (pbk.) |
    ISBN 9781315659947 (ebk)
Subjects: LCSH: School superintendents. | School board-
    superintendent relationships.
Classification: LCC LB2831.7 .W65 2017 | DDC 371.2/011—dc23
LC record available at https://lccn.loc.gov/2016036572

ISBN: 978-1-138-96117-3 (pbk)
ISBN: 978-1-315-65994-7 (ebk)

Typeset in Palatino
by Apex CoVantage, LLC

Contents

Meet the Authors

Ryan Donlan

Dr. Ryan Donlan helps leaders, teams, and organizations in all sectors toward personal and professional excellence. Schools and school leaders are his focus. Ryan is an Assistant Professor of Educational Leadership in the Bayh College of Education at Indiana State University in Terre Haute, Indiana. He leverages leadership capacity in others toward higher performance.

Prior to his university career, Ryan started as a high school teacher and served as an Assistant Principal, Principal, and Superintendent over many years in both traditional and non-traditional schools. Leadership development, school re-imagination, and organizational wellness are his specialties, as are human behavioral analysis and the study of personality and communication. Ryan is a practitioner's scholar, and a scholar's practitioner.

With wide-ranging publications and an expanding readership, Ryan is co-author of the books *Minds Unleashed: How Principals Can Lead the Right-Brained Way*, *The Secret Solution: How One Principal Discovered the Path to Success*, and author of the book *Gamesmanship for Teachers: Uncommon Sense is Half the Work*.

Ryan is married to Wendy, an early-childhood, infant-and-toddler educator, who is a teacher in the Early Childhood Education Center at Indiana State University. They are the parents of two children, Sean and Katelyn.

Todd Whitaker

Dr. Todd Whitaker has been fortunate to be able to blend his passion with his career. Recognized as a leading presenter in the field of education, his message about the importance of teaching has resonated with hundreds of thousands of educators around the world. Todd is a professor of educational leadership at the University of Missouri in Columbia, Missouri, and Professor Emeritus at Indiana State University in Terre Haute, Indiana. He has spent his life pursuing his love of education by researching and studying effective teachers and principals.

Prior to moving into higher education he was a math teacher and basketball coach in Missouri. Todd then served as a principal at the middle school, junior high, and high school levels. He was also a middle-school coordinator in charge of staffing, curriculum, and technology for the opening of new middle schools.

One of the nation's leading authorities on staff motivation, teacher leadership, and principal effectiveness, Todd has written over 40 books including the national best seller, *What Great Teachers Do Differently*. Other titles include *Your First Year, Shifting the Monkey, Dealing with Difficult Teachers, The 10 Minute Inservice, The Ball, What Great Principals Do Differently, Motivating & Inspiring Teachers*, and *Dealing with Difficult Parents*.

Todd is married to Beth, also a former teacher and principal, who is a faculty member in Educational Leadership at the University of Missouri and Professor Emeritus at Indiana State University. They are the parents of three children: Katherine, Madeline, and Harrison.

Acknowledgments

We would like to thank those who have served as our heroes, while we have worked to provide something relevant to our K-12 superintendents who make a positive difference in school districts every day. A special "thanks" to Superintendents Dr. David Hoffert and Rob Moorhead for their prepublication assistance and expertise with our manuscript. To our many friends, colleagues, and students at Indiana State University and the University of Missouri, we want you to know that we value your support and the encouragement you provide. Finally, to our wives and families, we send our gratitude and love for the continual inspiration you offer, as we are lucky guys, indeed.

1

The Hero Maker

The relationship between a school board and the superintendent is incredibly fascinating and complex. The superintendent is typically chosen and hired by a school board and then answers to this same leadership body. This seems simple enough. We get hired by a group and then also have to follow its leadership and expectations. Most jobs fall under this type of a structure. However, many factors make the dynamic between the superintendent and the school board much more complicated.

A board is not one person, which we can picture as a traditional "boss." Instead, it is a group of individuals that may or may not function together in a healthy or professional fashion. In addition, it may be a group whose membership is composed of changing people. A new superintendent might be selected unanimously by a five-member board and just months later, three new "bosses" are in place because an election resulted in a 60 percent turnover of the board. And these three new members may have a completely different vision

> A board is not one person, which we can picture as a traditional "boss." Instead, it is a group of individuals that may or may not function together in a healthy or professional fashion.

of what they want their superintendent to accomplish. Their vision may not just differ from that of the three members they replaced; it may also differ dramatically from that of the two existing members and from that of the other recently elected officials. This, in and of itself, is an incredible challenge. But amazingly, this may be the easy part.

What is really unique is that superintendents must then have the skills and abilities to actually lead their bosses. This delicate balance makes the superintendent–board relationship so complex. A trained and educated professional such as yourself must lead an organization under the guidance and supervision of people who potentially have little or no training or education in how to lead your organization. And simultaneously, they decide your fate. The quandary is that if you allow the board to tell you what to do, you may not be doing what is best for the organization, yet if the board isn't allowed to exercise its elected authority, their public is not getting what it wants, nor the representation that is provided for them under the law. Compounding this situation is the fact that as policymaking power has been taken from local communities, boards are often left focusing on the more minor issues, which get in the way of your leadership. If superintendents cannot solve this complex puzzle, it becomes almost impossible for them to be effective in promoting school success and leading the principals and teachers under their guidance. This book is designed to assist with this potentially scary tightrope walk.

Diversity in the Ranks

School board members may have incredibly varied backgrounds. Some may be former teachers, principals, or even previous superintendents. Within this group there can be past successful educators who get the "big picture" and work to help advance the district to do what is best for all students and staff. Also within this group may be someone who was fired by the school board at a previous time and who potentially has a desire to hold the current members, and even you, as a personal bull's-eye. Target-shooting is this person's biggest incentive to become a district leader.

Some school board members have successful businesses, farms, or professional practices, while others have nothing else to do. There may be individuals with five children currently enrolled in the district and others with zero. They can be volunteers or receive a lucrative stipend for their roles. There can be board members who have a district-wide perspective and others who have the goal of getting their nieces jobs as teachers. One member may be a lover of sports, and another may want the football coach fired because his son is not the starting running back. One may feel that cheerleading should have additional funding for new uniforms, and others may have the view that the spirit squad should be disbanded.

There may be members of the group who have advanced degrees and others who only graduated from the school of hard knocks. Some may have a wealth of common sense, and others may seem to have a dearth of it. Put all of these different perspectives and views together, and it can seem overwhelming. But the next challenge may be even more daunting. With no positional power over the board, the superintendent must be able to teach and influence these individuals to function together to make decisions based on what is best for the students and best for the school district. Being able to do this with no formal organizational advantage is a task that at times can seem challenging and even overwhelming. How is it possible to lead our bosses? Should we even attempt it? Are there more effective ways to do so?

Are There Any Commonalities?

Upon first reflection, it may seem an insurmountable task to *lead* this group of individuals down a common path when they potentially have such dramatically differing backgrounds and viewpoints. It can be difficult even to conceive of how to meld them into any type of cohesive group. Sometimes just getting them to "play nice" in public can be a challenge. Is there anything that we can do to influence those who are our employers, when we are in actuality the employees who are required to answer to them? How can we help them successfully sort through the many voices they hear from the public: from the club, the shop, and/or around the neighborhood card game?

We know why you might, at times, have a tight feeling in the pit of your stomach. Yet, we believe that you will be successful in this incredibly important position, despite the seemingly no-win playing field. You will do this by discovering some things that we all agree on.

Although it may seem that a group such as your board of education has such different members that it can't have a common ground, there *is* one thing these members share. All school board members want to make a difference for their particular groups of constituents. Or to put it another way, each member wants to be a hero. That's right, a hero. And your job is to help them accomplish this in a positive and productive fashion.

The board member who runs for the position to cut taxes, the member who has a goal of getting rid of the girls' basketball coach, and the member who wants to help pass a referendum or bond to build a new school, all have one shared outcome: They want to be heroes.

Now, you may be thinking that some of these viewpoints would actually make them lots of enemies, or would lead to harmful results. You may be correct. These members may have the minority viewpoint or may have an aim that common sense tells us would lead to more harm than good. But in their minds, if they accomplish what they set out to do, the result is they will be heroes to someone who matters to them.

One may feel like her daughter will be so proud of her if mom can get on the school board and get rid of the basketball coach who cut her "baby girl" from the squad in her sophomore year. Others may interact with a political group that wants to cut taxes, and if they can help make this happen, they will then be supported to run for a more significant office in the community. An individual could hope to be elected or appointed to the board so that funds can be raised to build a new high school that will positively impact future students and the community for generations to come.

Although in some ways their goals may seem contradictory in nature, the underlying aim is to be held in a more positive regard by others.

Although in some ways their goals may seem contradictory in nature, the underlying aim is to be held in a more positive regard by others.

For some members, these "others" might just be the people sitting around the dinner table in their dining room. Some board members might actually see the benefit of providing a better education for students and how that can benefit the community through a more educated population. And some members might seem to have a "real aim" that is obvious, but there is a chance they do not know what is their real purpose in serving.

Making Heroes

One task a superintendent must focus on is how to position these individual board members as heroes by helping them do the right thing instead of something else influenced by their own personal agendas, because their agendas may not be what is best for the students and the district. When we can accomplish this, we can then help those who are our supervisors come together in a more cohesive way to realize their goals of being heroes.

One of the primary purposes of this book is to help district leaders understand the importance of hero-making. A second and potentially more challenging aim is to help teach and develop the specific skills needed to accomplish this daunting task. To do this, we discuss, in the chapters ahead, the constituencies that influence board members and that fuel their desires to be heroes. We talk about boards of education and their responsibilities in our system of education. Since the superintendent's role is critical to the success of the board, we talk about how superintendents serve as a shield for boards, so that they are protected when they make the right decisions. We also discuss how the best board meetings are conducted, and what the superintendent should do between meetings so that school leadership functions well. Finally, we discuss the individual board members with whom superintendents come into contact, and how they are motivated to make decisions, no matter the communities in which they serve. We even show how superintendents can start undefeated each year—and for those who are considering a new challenge, we pose the question, "Is there a time to move on?"

If you are a district leader, you are highly aware of the incredible responsibility you have. Every day, your actions and decisions influence hundreds, or even thousands, of young people in your schools. You knew this responsibility when you chose your leadership role. You wanted to make a difference. Now we have to figure out how to make an impact, through the making of heroes. Your students deserve it. The final goal of this book is to help school leaders understand that making others into heroes accomplishes the same result for themselves. A true hero is someone who helps others accomplish things they didn't think were possible.

A true hero is someone who helps others accomplish things they didn't think were possible.

Thanks for what you do. Thanks for making a difference. Every day.

⭐ Hero-making Tips

- ◆ Hero makers make an honest appraisal and ask themselves: "What characteristics and behaviors do I have that influence those with authority over me to want to be led and taught by me?"
- ◆ Hero makers then ask that same question of someone who will tell them the truth.
- ◆ Hero makers ensure that board members are able to look backward with pride and forward with hope, in every conversation.
- ◆ Hero makers realize something that was shared with us recently by a friend of ours who is a superintendent: "There are two kinds of parents: board members and future board members." Each community member whom superintendents meet could someday be their boss, and hero makers act accordingly.

2

Constituencies

A superintendent has to keep an eye to the sky, much like an air traffic controller, with radar scanning to ensure that the right planes are landing at the right times, on the right runways, and at the right airports. We don't want people crashing into each other. The pilots are more aptly described as the powerbrokers in any given community whose job it is to carry passengers (those whom they serve) from one destination to another, typically from a place of "needing something" to a place of "getting something." The passengers associated with each powerbroker make up the constituencies, or groups, that influence the life of any superintendent.

Understanding Expectations

Each constituency has expectations.

We might have the Music Boosters constituency in one group, the Chamber of Commerce in another group, and the Teacher's Union in a third. What is fascinating about these constituencies is that in most cases, each one has a cause that they believe in, and taken separately, most of their causes by and large make sense.

Think about it this way: What's wrong with putting more resources into music? What's wrong with running schools more like a business, in terms of how dollars are spent and costs are contained? What's wrong with giving teachers a raise for the hard work that they do? Nothing really, if these issues or actions are taken separately. But these groups do not see the full picture. When groups become so ingrained that the only view they see or hear is a view similar to their own, it becomes challenging to expand their way of thinking.

Social media can compound this situation.

We would think that having access to the views of thousands of others could help us all learn and grow. Of course it could—*if* we were to interact with and appreciate those who have differing opinions than we do. However, if we only associate with like-minded people online or otherwise, not only do we believe we are correct, but we may also think that there isn't even another point of view at all.

This is not to indict social media. It is an important and incredibly valuable tool, but it does help us see how board members and other constituencies who only interact with those who share the same views can have a great deal of trouble seeing an alternative world. And believe us, these constituencies will be quick to point out what their world is all about, with no clue of its limitations. Their quick, negative comments provide an imbalanced view of any given situation.

But the fact remains that as stewards of the community dollar, superintendents have only so many resources to go around, and investing in one constituency typically brings an obligation to de-invest in another, unless you are going to spend money you don't have. Over time, this practice has a tendency to alienate people if not handled delicately, especially when everyone thinks that their "baby" is the cutest (and that by not paying special attention to it, you're calling it ugly).

Embracing Complication

With constituencies, things can get complicated.

To try to list all of the given constituencies that a superintendent needs to handle (and what to do about them) would be counterproductive here, because communities are all different. We can say, however, that anywhere you go, you will find a handful of constituencies and their motives will invariably contradict one another. Superintendents who did not forecast this never-ending state of contradiction were probably a bit naïve in the job search. The saving grace is that what *is* common in all communities is the fact there really is order within chaos. Constituencies do behave predictably. Because of this, superintendents have a great resource from which to establish focus and priority.

All they have to do is to study their boards of education.

After all, individual board members are often elected upon the shoulders of the constituencies who feel the most compelled to turn their feelings into action. They are often elevated to office by those who feel most strongly about issues affecting their children or community, and thus, make great informational conduits that superintendents can use to gather information, and then prioritize decision making. Superintendents must at times filter the information that board members bring to them, as some board members are only in tune with the perspectives of their particular group, yet even fringe information is valuable.

When meeting together, the board of education becomes its own living "constituency," as members coalesce and paint a clear picture of community sentiment. Boards of education become their own poster children of what should be "urgent" in a superintendent's life, and what should be "important."

Constituencies, Uncovered

As does any constituency, the board of education has the following characteristics:

1. It has issues that define it.
2. It has power and influence.
3. It has people.
4. It can behave irrationally.

Yet, more importantly:

5. It has a hierarchy of needs.
6. It wants to be a hero.

Think of the local group that wants to start a new academic tutoring program in your community, and they want it funded with tax dollars that currently go to your school. On the surface, one may hear them talk about issues of "family choice," "equity of opportunity," or a host of other issues that can define the group's agenda. It is pretty hard to argue with any of these issues because the underlying values seem to make sense. Of course, we would like to think we are already providing good tutoring to students, and maybe we are, but that's not the point.

A constituency is out there that feels differently.

The group might also have power or influence, which might include the backing of several prominent community members. At times, you might see some irrational behavior, such as zealotry or public criticism of you, with some scud missiles fired. All constituencies have a few crazies they keep around, to create helpful distractions for their own greater good.

Yet, what this group could also have, for sure, are needs.

The group, and its membership, has a need to be heard, and some of the individual members probably have not been heard in a long time, or at the minimum they feel that they haven't, which is just as relevant to them. They might have a need for peace at the dinner table or breakfast nook, and each day for the past ten years they have been fighting with their children to go to school. Maybe they have a need to keep the promise they made to their children that school will eventually get more tolerable for them, and currently they are unaware of how to ask for help. Maybe they are not too smart and don't recognize that your local school is providing wonderful tutoring and pays for the transportation to and from, yet what is really going on is that they have a need to be thought of as smart, in the eyes of their own children, for the first time in a long time.

Maybe they have a need to take a few shots at the principal, not because the principal is a bad guy, but because they had a loser principal 20 years ago and 100 miles away, and it is time to right the wrong that they felt, from their own backside. Behavior such as this is most typically related to personal experience in school.

Now these things might be 100 percent not your school district's fault, but they are needs nevertheless. They underlie the professed issue of tutoring. By the way, the constituency as a whole has a need, too. It has a need *to meet the needs* of its membership. In short, it needs to be a hero. Beyond their veneer, all groups are like fragile adolescents when it comes to their basic needs. Superintendents who understand that are in the best position to make a difference.

> **Beyond their veneer, all groups are like fragile adolescents when it comes to their basic needs. Superintendents who understand that are in the best position to make a difference.**

How Hero Makers Handle Them

Our best superintendents help promote the positive energy of constituencies, rather than working against their bad energy. They pay more (and positive) attention to those issues that are mutually agreeable among constituencies, and they provide less attention to those that cannibalize others' agendas. One might even say that hero-making superintendents help constituencies to exercise their good legs, and don't pay as much attention to the rehabilitating of the bad.

If the Boy Scouts and the local tobacco lobby share a common interest in helping the local humane society build a dog park, it will be the conversation topic around the campfire, and in the cigar shop too, most of the time. It is not so much a matter of "what" the superintendent pays positive attention to, it is "that" the superintendent is paying attention to something important to the constituency. Attention really is quantifiable, as is positive affirmation during those times together.

Paying attention and providing positive affirmation are really opportunities to treat people and their constituencies like heroes.

Our best superintendents work with their constituencies by starting with the "hero" (#6 from the constituency characteristics previously noted), forgiving in advance any irrationality they encounter and moving into addressing the real needs that people have—some that the people don't even realize—as they address their issues. Knowing that constituencies want to be heroes to those they represent, and board members want to be heroes to those constituencies, allows superintendents to better meet the groups' needs for safety, love, and belonging. Once these needs are met, the board becomes much more pliable, as do the constituencies, and are much less prone to dysfunction. Over time, through a superintendent's guidance and caretaking, these constituencies enhance their own power and influence to address positively the issues that are important to the constituency in the first place.

Smart superintendents are able to establish common ground so that their own issues, needs, and goals seem congruent with those of their constituencies, even when they are very different. They start with understanding and finding the need to be a hero in everyone, particularly in those on their boards, then moving through needs, to get to the people inside.

> **Smart superintendents are able to establish common ground so that their own issues, needs, and goals seem congruent with those of their constituencies, even when they are very different.**

Where this is particularly important is in the public recognition by the superintendent of the issues important to constituencies each and every year. We don't recommend that this is done through a town hall meeting with the expressed purpose stated and advertised. That would be like inviting a bunch of hungry cannibals to dinner. Instead, deft hero makers realize that the opportunity lies within the school improvement and strategic planning process. These annual planning and improvement meetings serve as an incredible opportunity to bring constituencies together for a conversation, and more importantly, for needs fulfillment (although never advertised as such), all the while improving schools along the way.

School Improvement-as-Constituency Leverage

Hero makers understand that building principals are the boots on the ground of any successful school improvement initiative. Yet, superintendents play a pivotal role in the overall coordination and strategic planning for school improvement assignments and activities district-wide. Consider the following: Critical to school improvement processes is to have a careful selection process of those members of certain constituencies that will attend. Hero makers realize that they need strong constituency representatives who are respected and connected within those groups, even among the crazies. Yet they do not want the crazies, of course, or those who are insecure or too weak to serve as an ambassador when reporting back to the group on what the school is doing, and how the school is giving consideration to the group's agenda.

In the best school improvement processes involving constituencies, the hero maker remains in charge of the venue, yet like an air-traffic controller, farming most of the piloting to others. Through the conversations that take place regarding how the school is doing and what it can be doing better, the hero maker asks key constituents to work alongside educators to make the school a better place. Equally important, by asking everyone in the room what issues are important to them with respect to education in the community, the hero maker is showing these people that they are important and valuable. A natural outgrowth are key assignments for members of certain committees, yet with the committee chairing best left to the educators.

Again, the school improvement process or strategic planning in any school district is certainly undertaken for the expressed purpose of improving one's schools, and this is a must-have and the bottom line. However, these processes in any school district can serve as a leverage point for meeting the needs of constituencies so that hero makers can actively work to ensure others' needs are met, and thus, bring out the best in constituencies and the people in them.

Hero-making Exists at All Levels

Although we are focusing on how board members all want to be heroes, never lose sight of the fact that so does everyone else. The movie *It's a Wonderful Life* resonates as a classic for lots of reasons, but one of them is that we all want to be important, remembered, and significant. In some part of everyone's heart is the desire to be "the biggest man in town." Who hasn't dreamed of being George Bailey at some point? We all dreamed when we were younger of scoring the winning basket, being the lead in the play, or nailing the dismount from the uneven parallel bars.

Our dreams may have changed, but they have not disappeared. Maybe it is catching that big fish, nailing a long putt in your Saturday golf scramble, or having a child say, "You are the best mom in the world," but whatever it is, it still resides in each of us.

The district leaders must also work to invite everyone feel significant and to make each employee feel special. As our skills develop, we can then apply them to new and more challenging situations. If we do not have the desire or ability to invite those we supervise to feel like heroes, we will probably not be able to invite those we work for to feel that way.

> If we do not have the desire or ability to invite those we supervise to feel like heroes, we will probably not be able to invite those we work for to feel that way.

By practicing these skills on a consistent basis, we are much more likely to have them become a part of our repertoire. By teaching those we supervise how to practice them as well, these approaches can help spread the warmth in our district. We need to find ways to teach our school building leaders (principals, directors, etc.) these same skills so that they can ensure the faculties and staffs in their care feel valued and important on a consistent basis.

Not only do we need to model this behavior on a consistent basis, but we must also intentionally develop these same skills in everyone that serves in a leadership role. Once this is infused throughout the building level, the principals can then help bring these same practices to the classrooms so that teachers can invite every student feel like a hero. As we build this as a culture in our district, it makes the next refer-endum we need to take to the voters in the community seem less daunting. Inviting others to feel like they are special helps them work harder and develop a much higher level of loyalty to our students, our schools, and ourselves.

> **Inviting others to feel like they are special helps them work harder and develop a much higher level of loyalty to our students, our schools, and ourselves.**

⭐ Hero-making Tips

- ◆ Hero makers ensure that as "air-traffic" controllers, they don't fly the plane. Their job is more about giving clear air space to others who have the controls.
- ◆ Hero makers understand that the best practical use of air-traffic controlling is to listen more and talk less; facilitate more and direct less; and remain above and outside the direct, play-by-play interchanges between building leaders and constituency representatives.
- ◆ Hero makers keep their noses to the wind for the next constituency that has an itch but is not getting scratched, because the board is not yet paying attention to it. This may be best done in coffee shops, the car mechanic's waiting room, the dental chair, or the barber shop/beauty salon. This is a prime opportunity to teach a board member to reach out and connect positively.
- ◆ Hero makers ensure that board members are a part of school improvement efforts, but don't necessarily assign them to the same committees with constituency representatives with whom they may have unhealthy ("unprotected") relationships.

3

The Board of Education

Boards of education typically have the plenary power (total power) to conduct the school's business locally. One problem is that in many cases, they operationalize their authority in ways that go beyond what an optimal working relationship would provide. This chapter presents a model that works, one that hero-making would help to foster.

Under ideal circumstances, the board of education has four main job descriptions: (1) hire and fire the superintendent, (2) set policy, (3) act on the budget, and (4) represent community sentiment. Beyond these, our best boards get out of the way and let the superintendents do what they do best—lead. Other boards see the need to get their fingers into places they don't belong, whether it is through micromanagement or throwing their titles around individually.

Superintendents tell us that it is hard to address issues of micromanagement, because board members sometimes take offense at the critical conversations that arise because of it. We don't believe there is any upside to addressing these circumstances *through the front door* with direct conversation having to do with something board members "should stop doing." After all, underlying a board member's nose getting stuck into the school's daily operations is a need that is not currently being met. Addressing the behavior without addressing the underlying need is just silly and, at best, a temporary solution.

One need of the board member is, as we have mentioned, to be a hero—possibly to keep a promise made to someone or an obligation felt to the core of one's existence. How can we compete with that? Well, we cannot, without getting on the same side as the board member—not on the side of their micromanagement, but on the side of scratching their itch, so to speak.

Meeting a person's need is really not that complicated but requires finesse and a genuine desire to understand that person, to bring about a conversion to the behavior we would want.

How Optimal Working Relationships Happen

The optimal working relationship between boards of education and superintendents starts ideally as soon as the superintendent is hired or maybe even during the interview, because this is where the superintendent has typically one win (the job) and no losses (the job). It may be the last time you feel undefeated, so milk it while you can!

Yet it can start anytime, really. It just gets harder to establish, the longer the relationship is not optimal.

One main strategy is necessary to fostering positivity: Make time to reach out and stay connected to board members individually, as often as they need reassurances that their voices are heard, loud and clear. Whether this is a morning coffee at their workplace, a lunch "on the superintendent" (not the district), or on the sidelines of a soccer field, it is critical for superintendents to prioritize this time with board members individually.

Make time to reach out and stay connected to board members individually, as often as they need reassurances that their voices are heard, loud and clear.

During these meetings, if the board member is talking much more than the superintendent, the visit is doing what the visit is supposed to do. It is critical for the superintendent to casually mention what the optimal relationship would be, without talking about an optimal relationship. The more you listen to someone, the smarter they think you are. Here is an example:

> *You know, Cathy, one of the things that I always keep in mind is not to veer from the policy decisions you and the board make. Once you all provide the guardrails for how we operate, I make it my mission to handle the details for you. You can count on me. I always appreciate, as well, your taking the time to share your concerns, as it allows me to better understand what's important.*

Another example:

> *Hey, the one thing that I can assure you, Bob, is that I know who my boss is—seven great people who get together once a month. Whatever you vote on that night, whether it is policy, budget, or even my contract, you can rest assured that I'll take care of all the details. The last thing you need on your plate is the minutia.*

A Delicate Lesson to Learn

One important point that board members probably should learn, *through the side door*, is that they only really have the authority to do what they do when they meet as a group. Individually, they do not have official authority to do anything. They cannot come into your buildings and boss your principals around; they cannot give teachers orders or tell coaches who is going to start on the basketball team.

Okay, we realize some of you may be saying, "They sure can!"

And you are right, when things *aren't* right. We bet there are a lot of you out there who have found yourself in those circumstances.

The point is that board members really *should not*, since most often under the law they do not have the power. Hero makers understand how to get this behavior under control, without having to quote song and verse of state statute. In ideal circumstances, the board will somehow learn these things through the professional development opportunities you provide them or through the informational materials the statewide school board association shares, or even better through the casual conversations you have with them as you prioritize your time, one-on-one.

As an aside—one thing that we will discuss later in the book is that when a superintendent organizes a professional development experience for board members, the superintendent should always attend as a learner himself or herself. Rather than nod or point out a board member's faux pas when the outsider provides direction, we can and should be a peer and act like it is *new knowledge* for us to learn as well. Rather than giving the impression that we knew something they did not, it may be better to help everyone feel that we are all learning this simultaneously. This can prevent insecurities from arising, which can dampen building a collaborative relationship between and among board members and administrators.

Using language such as, "Someone suggested that we might . . ." or "The other day I heard an idea . . ." can be much more palatable and can build collaborative relationships much more than "Do you know something I thought of . . ." or "I think we should. . . ." Taking the approach that we are all learning at the same time and making everything be someone else's idea can lower the guard or defensiveness at key times.

Noted again, a model that truly works is when boards of education hire the superintendent, set the policy, authorize a budget, share community sentiment, and then let the superintendent lead. And yes, an occasional whisper about what this group wants, or what the group is worried about, is helpful for board members to relay, though much-better shared with the superintendent in a coffee shop at 7 am than through grandstanding at a board meeting.

There is nothing worse than when every board member wants his or her remarks entered into their own personal Congressional Record during a board meeting, especially when the newspaper reporter or television station stops by. That only perpetuates a model of governance (and leadership) that does not work, because rather than listening, too many are just awaiting a pause in the jabbering to interject what they want to interject.

I'm Just Looking Out for You

Helping board members do the right thing because it is in best interest is an essential element to the training process. we've said, it's important to share with them, from the beginning of your tenure with them or as new board members join the team, how they should not have to spend their valuable time dealing with trivial details.

> Helping board members do the right thing because it is in *their* best interest is an essential element to the training process.

For example, if board members receive a call from an upset parent, they should not have to take their valuable time trying to resolve it. Feel free to encourage the board members to have the parent call you directly so that they do not have their evening spoiled by some minor concern someone tries to drop in their lap. And then make yourself available to field the call, which is an important caveat to this offer on your part. When you get the call, you can redirect it to the appropriate building leader, after providing a listening ear.

Now, what if it is something the board members want to be a part of—if it is something they feel will make them a hero, if they can resolve it? Help them understand that although this time it may be something they are interested in—i.e. the football team coach selection (pet project for a specific board member, let's say)—they really don't want to deal with it because the next call might be about the pompon squad tryouts or National Honor Society inductions, and they might not want to get caught up there!

Help them understand that whatever ground-level action they take (or how low they go on the organizational food chain) to solve or address an issue, this action becomes the standard for which they will have to address all issues. In other words, if they decide to try to have a three-day suspension overturned, no school administrator will want to make a decision at that level in the future because it might be overturned and result in a public embarrassment for the school-level leader.

In addition, the school board has now sent a message to the community that if they do not like a building-level decision that involves a three-day suspension or any discipline comparable, they can just bring it to the board's attention, and the board will "fix" it for them. Help them understand that while doing it this one time may move them up temporarily on someone's hero meter, it runs the risk of forcing them to make potentially unpopular decisions on a regular basis, which will have the opposite long-term result.

Although this time they may feel heroic, help them foresee what can be forthcoming as a result of this decision. Reassure them that you value their input privately, but that the parents who complained are better served when they understand that it was not the board member who made the final decision.

Also, teach the board member that when hearing parental or community complaints, even any personal commentary or an eye roll can put them in a bad situation in the future. Saying things like, "We'll take care of this for you!" when a parent shares a story can be all the spark needed to set off a powderkeg of fireworks in the future. Hero makers teach their board members that once they get down and wrestle in the mud, they will be expected to do so time and again, and sooner or later, they will want to opt out of the match, and this will be awkward for them.

Hero makers teach their board members that once they get down and wrestle in the mud, they will be expected to do so time and again, and sooner or later, they will want to opt out of the match, and this will be awkward for them.

Although we mention that it would put the board member in a bad situation in the future, it obviously puts superintendents in an equally bad or worse situation. We know this. However, we also know that the board members may or may not care if they cause you future struggles, but for sure they do not have any interest in adding to their own personal grief down the road.

That is why hero makers plant these seeds with their boards. It pays to remind them that if they as board members mishandle an issue even once, those same board members will potentially be the ones that deal with all of the anger and unhappiness as future decisions mount. We want to keep them off this trajectory. And we want them to appreciate that from us. As hero makers, if we do not start with teaching our superiors, we will find ourselves in situations where we have all of the responsibility and none of the corresponding authority, and this is an incredibly stressful dynamic from which to try to lead.

The Delta Force

Before we close this chapter, we should mention the need for a Delta Force of Leadership, as written about in *Minds Unleashed: How Principals Can Lead the Right-Brained Way* (Donlan & Gruenert, 2016). Applied to hero making, it is when three important entities *do things right*: the superintendent, the board, and the board president. If these three are doing their jobs well, things typically go well in terms of school governance.

Again, the board's role is what we have described in this chapter (policy, budget, etc., as the "what"); the superintendent's (leading and managing) is more the "how." The board president has a special role in that he or she helps the other two groups establish four components necessary for a good relationship: trust, deference, assurance, and humility (Donlan & Gruenert, 2016).

Trust. Superintendents must trust that their boards represent accurately what their communities want from their schools;

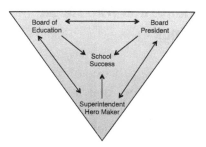

FIGURE 3.1 The Relationship between the Hero Maker, Board of Education, and School Board President for Optimal Governance and School Success

Source: Donlan & Whitaker, extending Delta Force of Leadership (Donlan & Gruenert, 2016) to Hero Making.

boards must trust superintendents to handle the details. Boards must trust that their board president and superintendent communicate often enough (ideally weekly) (Donlan & Gruenert, 2016). When boards feel like heroes, trust is easier to maintain.

Deference. Boards must be willing to defer day-to-day operations to superintendents; superintendents must defer to boards when policies need to be made (Donlan & Gruenert, 2016). Both boards and superintendents must defer the operational details of the schools to their building principals, and instructional decisions to the teachers and staff (Donlan & Gruenert, 2016). Consider how much easier it is for a hero to show appropriate deference, than it is for a non-hero.

Assurance. Board presidents should give assurances to superintendents that their day-to-day authority will not be questioned. Superintendents should provide assurances to board presidents that weekly updates will occur. Board members would ideally provide assurances that they will not intentionally micromanage school operations (Donlan & Gruenert, 2016). We contend that boards who feel like heroes have the confidence to provide assurances.

Humility. Everyone together must realize with humility that mutual support is the key to a positive relationship (Donlan & Gruenert, 2016). As hero making allows for confidence building, boards can better demonstrate humility.

Ideal Board Governance and Who Should Attend Board Meetings

Board governance—or its process of making decisions toward better outcomes for the school district—ideally starts with board members who realize the power and opportunity in their staying above the fray (operations). It allows them the opportunity not to feel that they must provide kneejerk assurances to their hardware store customers or to the patients in their practices who share their concerns.

In fact, a board that spends its time on minutia (the sprint) is actually abrogating its responsibility to quality governance (the marathon). This reminds us of the sage wisdom we received when we were young and were ascending the educational food chain, regarding how long people have to make decisions. Teachers are bound to respond to something in the moment. Assistant principals sometimes have the luxury of a bit more investigation. Principals can schedule a meeting to levy a decision on most things, and superintendents can wait a bit longer, because they may want to gauge how different constituencies will react.

A board that spends its time on minutia (the sprint) is actually abrogating its responsibility to quality governance (the marathon).

Board members, in terms of their governance and leadership, actually have the luxury of sharing with constituents that they would be happy to bring up their rapid-fire concerns at the next board work session. Doing so might make a good percentage of the angst go away naturally, if mindful follow-up accompanies it, of course, but also it allows board members to focus more on the larger issues that superintendents rely on them for:

- Policy changes that may affect the district for the next decade;
- Curricular adoptions that could make a powerful difference in the skills children take with them into higher education;
- Staffing decisions that may be with the school for the next 30 years;
- Approval of purchases that enable moving their missions toward visions;
- Community sentiment, in terms of infrastructure and support for facilities;
- Statutory developments that may influence how policies are prioritized and resources utilized.

These issues are the stratospheric issues that must be thought of deliberately, prudently, and deeply by some really great minds indeed. Although it seems that at times, pedestrians win elections, hero makers are effective at allowing board members to realize the large import placed on their time and talent. If they are kept focused on handling the heavyweight issues, these will take their time and energy, so it behooves the hero maker to help board members understand who must handle the community's light work.

The differences in time span available for making decisions as we move up the food chain is one reason we need to think if we want board meetings to include members of building leadership, such as principals and assistant principals. Although it makes for a nice way to have building reports reach the board, having the building administrators present during community remarks can be a bit more tenuous. Potshots can be taken. This can be awkward for members of the board, whom we are trying to keep as heroes. Boards may feel obligated to request immediate responses for accusations tossed. This puts good people on the line, without much time to deflect, and it can even get legally complicated.

Having building administrators excused from board meetings by the time community remarks are offered can go a long way toward defusing the issue. In such, the board president or superintendent can then say to the aggrieved party, "This can be looked into by the principal." If building leaders must be present because that is simply the way business has been done in your community, it pays to coach your building administrators not to offer any answers at a public board meeting, but rather to acknowledge the concerns and offer to meet privately with the concerned party to fully discuss the issue.

We understand there may be times when the superintendent wishes the transportation director, head of maintenance, or principal were at a meeting to answer a question from a board member or provide information in response to a public inquiry. However, there may be times that the superintendent is glad they are not there, so that a time lapse can be used to our benefit to gather information and prepare an appropriate and consistent response.

We find that weaker superintendents often allow their leadership team to get horsewhipped at board meetings, so that they themselves are insulated. Hero makers certainly do not do that, because this is not what effective leaders do. They are aware that in all situations they are ultimately responsible, so they work to protect their employees by keeping them off the front lines whenever possible. Superintendents and their teams have enough responsibility and pressure on a daily basis. There is no reason to heighten it at a public hearing. Plus, if our building leaders do not provide an immediate and satisfactory response, there may be more damage control than we might wish.

Hero makers know that when a person shares something during the open forum, asking that person to contact you tomorrow can be a way to sift out how important it is to him or her. If your phone is ringing at 8:00 the next day, it must really matter to that person. If you never hear from him or her again, that may also indicate how pressing it was. This does not mean that you do not follow up, but it may help to frame the essential nature of their issue. As with many negative people, they jump from issue to issue so quickly that if we can put off a response for even a few hours or days, they have moved on to something else.

⊛ Hero-making Tips

◆ Hero makers clearly articulate an optimal board/superintendent relationship at their job interview in terms of the four clear roles of the board (the "what"), and leadership expectations of the superintendent (the "how"). They then look closely, without appearing that they are, for the board's reaction, to gauge agreement on good governance, and whether or not they want the job.

◆ Hero makers master the facial expressions, tones, and gestures that are needed to have critical conversations with their boards on the advantages they can accrue from not making promises or making knee-jerk reactions when angry people call them. They are able to convey sincere worry for the board members, almost whispering in their ear convincingly about the problems that meddling will cause them personally, and how we "have their back" through another way.

◆ Hero makers protect their leadership team from potshots at board meetings, by ensuring that they are one-step removed from public scud missiles and board-level inquisitions. This protects all parties and helps boards in their roles as heroes.

Reference

Donlan, R., & Gruenert, S. (2016). *Minds Unleashed: How Principals Can Lead the Right-Brained Way*. Lanham, MD: Rowman & Littlefield Education.

4

The Superintendent as The Shield

In terms of their election or appointment to a school board, board members put themselves out there in a sense, in a way that exposes them to critique and consternation. Friends, neighbors, clients, and customers all see them in a new role. And by virtue of some strange circumstance, it seems that everyone who has gone to school believes they are experts at knowing how schools should be run. Restaurants and schools have a lot in common. We have all been in them so we all think we can run them ourselves. That is probably one reason that the most common business to open is a restaurant. The fact that it is not nearly as easy to run a restaurant or lead a school as we might envision is probably the reason that the most common business to close is also a restaurant.

Non-educators thinking they know how to run schools is really as odd as our thinking we are expert plumbers, just because we used the toilet this morning. Yet, that is what we deal with constantly, and that is why board members need our protection.

Non-educators thinking they know how to run schools is really as odd as our thinking we are expert plumbers, just because we used the toilet this morning. Yet, that is what we deal with constantly.

We would like to introduce a few metaphors in leadership and governance that involve bows, arrows, quivers, and shields. It seems like everyone nowadays is carrying around their bows, arrows, and quivers—ready to shoot at school officials. Critical to our awareness, however, should be the public's readiness to shoot at our board members as well. Oh, and even in cases where they are not planning to shoot, we really should want our board members to think that they are ready to do so.

Here's why.
The superintendent is The Shield.
And, we want our board members to *believe this*!
A healthy bit of uncertainty is good for the soul.

Think about a situation in which a board member comes to us, demanding that we hire his new son-in-law as the coach of our basketball team. Well, actually we haven't fired the current coach yet, but the board member is certainly going to be demanding we do this at the next board meeting. He might even mention he has begun passing around a petition for others to sign.

Well, you and I know that the actual thing going on is that the board member probably has some personal or family dynamics that are influencing him. There may even be things he doesn't want aired in public that have to do with the situation.

The board member would rather make an issue of something that is probably not the reality than disclose his or her ulterior motive, which is personal in nature. In these situations, the hero maker would be the one to actually help out the board member.

Time for your cape and superpowers—enter The Shield.

In a private meeting prior to the board meeting, in a one-on-one conversation with the hurting board member, this may be said:

Superintendent: "Carl, first I want to thank you for having the district's back by lining up another basketball coach, in the wake of your idea about our team's need to head in a new direction with leadership. And it is very nice that you may already have identified a potential replacement."

Realizing, of course, that in his gut he knows what he is doing is actually based in personal baggage, the board member might say, "I'm simply here to do what's right by our kids, as that is what we're all here for, right?"

Superintendent: "Absolutely (sidling up to the board member [Whitaker, 2015]). You know, the one thing that I think is critical when our board has these difficult conversations is for me to keep a watch on how folks are going to react. It's one thing when they have a concern about me; it's another thing when they point in the direction of you all with a problem. That's not fair to you."

Board Member: "We can handle it; that's what we were elected to do."

Superintendent: "And I respect that. The one thing I might be concerned about here, is not so much *what* the board might consider doing, it's *when* the board might consider doing it."

Board Member: "The sooner the better would be best. We still have some season left. Do you know that some parents have told me their boys haven't played all season? That's ridiculous! We're here to be all about kids. This isn't the NCAA!"

Superintendent: "You do make a good point, and great minds think alike, as my leadership team had a conversation about just that. Knowing where you stood on this, I had them look into what was up with playtime equity. You know what I found out?"

Board Member: "No, what?"

Superintendent: "I found out that every boy who has made all practices this season, plus those who had pre-excused absences when they had to miss, have actually played in each game, and players other than the starting five are actually playing 45 percent more than they were in years past. Our coach was mindful of his evaluation by the athletic director last year where this was proposed as a growth area, and it looks as in doing so, he has built capacity, and we have our first chance of winning the division in eight years."

Member: "Well, what about [specific student's name]?"

Intendent: "I can't discuss that one in detail, as you know because we're still investigating, but I can share with you that you might very well be having a closed session conversation regarding the discipline for a group that was caught at a hotel party two weekends ago by local police, with alcohol. Very sorry but I need to protect you from any details at this time, because I'll be relying on your sound advice when we're together formally. Can you understand that?"

Board Member: "Just as long as you bring us all the facts."

Superintendent: "Of course I will, and what worries me the most in this situation is that I don't want the board to be put in a position where the other guy has a bazooka, and you all only have a slingshot, you included. Look, I know you have done your homework and have a great guy ready to step up and coach. What I'm more worried about is the fact that someone may feel you have a personal vendetta and that it had nothing to do with basketball. I do not want you to end up looking like the bad guy here."

Superintendent: "Can you imagine, heaven forbid, if the board went after a winning coach now, with a good deal of parental support from those whose kids are at practice, and someone starts accusing you on social media of seeking revenge? We do not want you to be depicted as the bad guy in this, or any, situation. I fear it won't work out well for you, or for the board."

The challenge is continually educating and reminding the board that we must have consistency in how we operate.

The challenge is continually educating and reminding the board that we must have consistency in how we operate. It is difficult to choose to go rogue in this case, but we want the district administrators to handle the situation next time. Reminding the board members how important and valuable they are as visionary leaders can help elevate them from dealing with things that will eventually lead to dysfunction for the school district.

✪ Hero-making Tips

◆ Hero makers work actively to manage positive relationships at all levels of their organization and community so that people tell them things in confidence. That way, they know what arrows might be launched against their board members, or what should be mentioned to their board members as possibilities, and can then emerge as The Shield.

◆ Hero makers do not run frantically from board member to board member with little shields each time they are about to step in traffic. The trick is to use shields judiciously to leverage the more important outcomes that you wish to achieve, not simply to handle every bit of "incoming" that seems urgent at the time.

Reference

Whitaker, T. (2015). *Dealing with Difficult Teachers*. (3rd ed.) New York, NY: Routledge.

5

The Care and Feeding
of Board Members

Superintendents are in a unique position in that they are employed by boards of education to lead all aspects of school district operations, yet in a strange way, they also act as an educational parent to the board itself. This dynamic occurs because the superintendent is the one who has been schooled in the trade knowledge associated with running an educational institution, and the board might very well not have been. Some board members might actually be clueless about the demands of contemporary school districts, with their only expertise being the fact that they made it through the 12th grade themselves.

Thus, much like a child's first teacher is his or her parent, a board member's first teacher is ideally the school superintendent. This is odd, in that board members are writing the superintendent's paycheck, yet it is still a fact. And just as in parent-child relationships, the burden of the responsibility of the care and feeding of children rests with the parent; in this case it is the superintendent who is responsible for the care and feeding of his or her board.

Hero-making superintendents do this exceptionally well . . . most of all, by *not* overthinking it.

Care

Superintendents provide for the care of their boards, very simply, by ensuring that their lower-order needs are met before encouraging that their higher-order needs be met. We've all learned about this need from Abraham Maslow, an American psychologist known widely for creating a hierarchy of needs. Maslow's theory denotes that a hierarchy of needs exists in all of us, and before our higher-order needs can be met, our lower-order needs must be satisfied. The first needs are physiological, then involve safety and security, and then have to do with belonging and love, then self-esteem, toward eventual and hopeful self-actualization. A visual of this hierarchy is shown here:

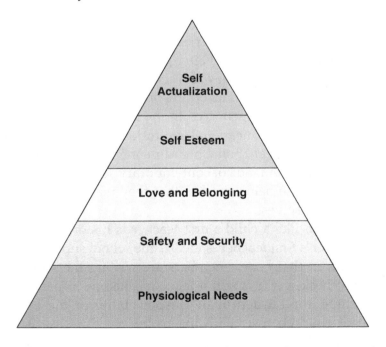

FIGURE 5.1 Visual Depiction of Abraham Maslow's Hierarchy of Needs

Source: Originally published in Maslow, A. (1943). A Theory of Human Motivation. *Psychological Review*, 50(4), 370–396.

We understand that new layers of needs have been added to Maslow's model in recent years (such as cognitive needs, aesthetic needs, and transcendence needs), yet for simplicity's sake, Maslow's original pyramid will suffice.

Physiologically—and with respect to safety and security needs—hero makers ensure that at every juncture, board members' service and the decisions that they make are going to be safe for their livelihoods and families. As we noted, superintendents serve as shields, by protecting their board members from public criticism and discontent. Imagine if the superintendent allowed for a partnership of the school district with a new-to-town, big-box retailer, in a way that would put the local hardware store owner/board member out of business. Or imagine if the superintendent steered the board in a direction that was so unpopular that local folks boycotted board members' businesses. That would not do any good for the care of any board member.

Hero makers do not lead their boards astray. They know what is both "safe" and "unsafe" for their board members and work toward doing what is right by the children of the school district, yet at the same time having their board members' backs while doing it. They need to anticipate what is going to cause a problem for individual board members, even if those board members do not anticipate the problem themselves or dismiss it.

That is just what hero makers do.

Feeding

Not ignoring other areas just as critical, hero makers who are effective with their boards are often working in overdrive to feed the board members in Maslow's areas of love, belonging, and self-esteem. Believe it or not, nearly all board members are on boards for these two reasons, which makes sense to us in that folks who feel like heroes are, by definition, loved and belong, with self-esteem a natural byproduct.

Hero makers who are effective with their boards are often working in overdrive to feed the board members in Maslow's areas of love, belonging, and self-esteem.

Hero Makers and Love and Belonging

Areas for love and belonging include those of friendship, family, intimacy, and a sense of connection. Hero makers know how important these are to board members and work to create situations in which board members feel like they matter, both professionally and personally.

Board members who feel "loved" see their pictures when they walk into the district's schools. They feel loved when receptionists know who they are and refer to them by name. They feel loved when they are constantly introduced in public as selfless individuals who are the real keys to everything positive that has happened in the district.

Hero makers ensure that board members' photographs are visible on websites and publications that are present in school offices, waiting rooms, and hallway tables. Board members feel loved when they get cards, paintings, and drawings by students. Board members feel loved when the basketball team brings them autographed schedule posters to hang in their dens or home offices. Hero makers ensure that they work with their principals so that there is a planned, yet quiet, rotation of care packages that come to all board members from children at strategic times of the year.

Yes, hero makers orchestrate expressions of love.

Board members "belong" when they arrive at a board meeting and are greeted warmly by the superintendent and secretary. They belong when smiling faces make conversation with them prior to the call to order—from principals, teachers, staff, and others in attendance. Board members belong when the superintendent knows enough about them and their particular interests, so that principals and teachers send invitations to them for classroom visits and special events. One board member might feel very much at home in the music room; another might love to tour the culinary arts or building trades programs. Board members experience belonging when hero makers know enough about them to know what makes them feel right at home.

Yes, hero makers orchestrate belonging as well.

Hero Makers and Self-Esteem

Areas of self-esteem include confidence, achievement, respect from others, and the need to be valued as a unique individual. Hero makers know how important these needs are for their boards. They strategically plan to mention particular board members and past accomplishments at certain times during each monthly meeting's agenda. They ensure that board members hear about other board members' accomplishments during discussions so that each member can look backward with pride and forward with hope, as Robert Frost once wrote (though admittedly, not about school boards). Being affirmed in front of others builds self-esteem.

Board members also experience a boost in self-esteem when superintendents echo and contextualize their remarks during board discussions. The last thing board members want is to make a point, then have the discussion abruptly move in a different direction. When this happens, they don't feel heard, and they can even be embarrassed. Hero makers serve as *human transitional phrases* to ensure smooth segues in conversation when some people just need to be quiet for a while, maybe saying things such as, *"And you know, Angela does make an excellent point in that one of our goals should be to ensure that the junior varsity parents are just as able to see their children's competitions from their bleachers as the varsity parents . . . and that is why it is particularly important that we hear from Robert, who shares that concern but wishes to note something that we as a group may need to consider as well."*

An interesting byproduct that we believe has a bit to do with the self-esteem of a board member is that of self-efficacy.

Self-efficacy is the belief that we can make a positive impact through hard work and earned effort. Self-efficacy is critical for positive board leadership and sound governance. Board members who have self-efficacy tend not to be insecure—not to delve quickly into conspiracy theories or rant about the haves and the have-nots at board meetings or on social media. They tend to stay away from playing the victim, and from helicoptering and

Hero makers know that the path toward fostering self-efficacy may come through self-esteem, in that one might need to feel good about oneself before believing that one is capable of setting goals, executing strategies, and making things happen.

rescuing. With self-efficacy, board members have a healthy sense of personal and professional autonomy and rather than bring about more problems, they tend to roll up their sleeves—whether in conversation or action—and do the critical work of governance with authenticity and compassion for those around them. Hero makers know that the path toward fostering self-efficacy may come through self-esteem, in that one might need to feel good about oneself before believing that one is capable of setting goals, executing strategies, and making things happen.

Hero makers also teach all of the district's administrators to thank, acknowledge, and build the importance of school board members. Through a trickle-down effect, effective building leaders help their faculty and staff members do the same. Not only does this assist with board relations, it also teaches others how to build effective relations in all aspects of their leadership. The superintendents also help administrators learn that issues and concerns are not to be directed to board members but rather to the appropriate district-level leader. This may seem like something that should inherently be known, and it probably should be, but if we do not help teach and educate our own employees about proper protocol, we may find ourselves wishing that we had!

Board members are really no different from the rest of us, and over the course of our lives, we have all experienced the need to be cared for and fed. This still continues, if we are to be honest about it.

★ Hero-making Tips

- Hero makers strike a balance in their relationships with board members. Like good parents, they do not want to be too standoffish, or the relationship doesn't flourish, yet they do not want to be too much of a friend either, in that their children (board members) won't think they can learn too much from them.
- Hero makers encourage board members to seek guidance from them when things get difficult, because they can be trusted for safety and security.
- Hero makers know how to have discussions with board members that do not mention "them" (board members), but really are about them. This has to do with having their back. Instead of mentioning how the consequences of a particular board action could adversely affect a particular board member's business or family, a hero maker would use a circumstance that is similar, or an "Imagine if . . ." so that the board member can make this extrapolation for himself or herself.
- Hero makers frame discussions and critical conversations so that board members feel any intended angst quietly on the inside (and then go home that evening thinking about it).
- Hero makers use numbers to their advantage and ensure that others in their school district know how to provide care and feeding as well. Many hands make for lighter work, and when feeding is occurring at all levels, the less the superintendent has to do individually. Why would one want to be seen running around the dinner table pouring everyone's glass of milk, when the milk can be passed around?
- Hero makers, through their actions, show board members how to provide for the care and feeding of other board members.

6

Board Meetings

Board meetings are meetings held by the policy makers and budget-setters of the school district to conduct the board's business. They are not town hall meetings. They are not intended to be meetings where the board micromanages aspects of school operations better left to its managers and leadership team. Rather, they are meetings where a group of duly elected community representatives come together to provide thoughts, perspectives, guidance, leadership, and supervision on whether or not the school is operating within the guidelines established by policy, whether the budget is being spent wisely, and whether or not the superintendent is doing his or her job as the chief operating officer.

It is a lesser-known fact that board meetings are the only time that board members have legitimate leadership authority under many state statutes. When a quorum is held, as per the board's bylaws or state law, the board can then act to conduct business. This is much different than the perception by some that board members, any time they wish, can show up in school buildings, park their vehicles where they wish, tell principals what to do, and show up in teachers' classrooms to see what is going on. In those instances, board members are actually community members, just like anyone else, and if community members cannot do it, board members should not be doing it either.

We may assume that all board members know this, but realistically how could they? Part of our responsibility is to teach them what is appropriate. Outside consultants can be used to provide these lines of demarcation to the board as well.

We recall instances where seemingly "crazy" board members visited the buildings of some of our friends and tried to stir up trouble. One board member tried to get teachers to fill out a petition of "No Confidence for the Superintendent." Another story we heard from a colleague concerned a board member showing up in the woodshop to use a tool for a home renovation project. Yet another board member we heard about loved to accompany the drug dogs through the lockers, not realizing that he really didn't have the right to conduct a search.

> **Board meetings are important in ensuring that the best decisions are made, that the best practices of discussion and deliberation are followed, and especially that every board member leaves the building feeling better than before he or she arrived.**

The point here is that board of education meetings are the only *real* time that board members have actual authority, and they occur either once a month, twice a month, or quarterly in more rare instances. Therefore, board meetings are important in ensuring that the best decisions are made, that the best practices of discussion and deliberation are followed, and especially that every board member leaves the building feeling better than before he or she arrived.

You might have guessed it. The superintendent's job is to ensure that each board member who walks out feels like a hero.

Here is what hero makers do to ensure that each board meeting goes better than the last one.

Creature Comforts

During board meetings, is the environment inviting? Are the parking lots plowed and the walks swept? Is someone cheerful (possibly a student) standing at the entrance of the administration building or school to greet board members as they arrive? Do board members see pictures of themselves at the entranceway, almost as if they were present members of a country club or even better . . . past presidents? Does the place smell inviting?

If the meeting is held in a school, do board members see the custodians still mopping the hallways near where the board meets or if the garbage is still being emptied, bags sitting in the hallway? We hope not. If this is still going on, someone is probably not doing a good job, and that someone is the superintendent (because the principal is not doing his or hers). It is critical to have an impeccable, inviting walkway, from each board member's vehicle all the way to the board member's seat at the board table.

Is dinner prepared? Not necessarily one paid for by the school district, but a small, inviting dinner prepared by the superintendent or others willing to do it voluntarily? Homemade soups are a nice touch, as are hors d'oeuvres and finger foods. You don't want something too sloppy, but something just enough to tide over board members if they have come directly from work and did not have time to stop for a bite to eat.

How about coffee and tea—decaf and regular? Small bottles of water are nice, or even a glass pitcher of water infused with cucumber, lemon, or orange.

Are board members seated in comfortable chairs, in a place where they are comfortable sitting? Do board members have nice nameplates in front of where they sit so that the public visiting can know who they are (but more importantly, so that each member can feel important by having a nameplate)? Does the arrangement of the board table and chairs allow for conversation? In other words, do the outside tables angle slightly inward, so that board members can communicate not only with each other but also with the public?

As a hero maker, your positioning is key. You want to be able to gauge the perceptions of each board member during the meeting from where you are sitting. It might be nice if you sit alongside the board president, so that you can whisper something in his or her ear if needed.

Is adequate space and positioning provided so that board members can stand up, sit down, and stand up again, and are they able to refill beverages or appetizer plates without disrupting other board members or getting between the board and the public? Might be nice to allow board members a special grazing area that is comfortable to navigate.

Finally, do you have someone positioned and on-hand to tend to any needs board members might have? For example, there might be a need for an additional photocopy, for an extra pen or highlighter, for flip charts, or for someone to refill beverages.

If you do, it might go a long way in meeting their needs.

Often, board members will leave a meeting not necessarily remembering everything that was said—but they will certainly remember if their needs were provided for, and how they felt.

> Board members will leave a meeting not necessarily remembering everything that was said—but they will certainly remember if their needs were provided for, and how they felt.

Hero makers proactively tend to the setting, and ensure that the setting is optimal, including everything that is within eyesight or earshot from the time board members step out of their car to the time they step back in it.

Is the arrangement of which board members are seated next to one other, or not, cleverly conceived and designed? Have you ever been at a meeting where a small (we hope) faction or group of naysayers felt more comfortable because they had the emotional support of proximity? Although this may not be something you can quickly change, you can consider it as new members join or different officers are elected.

Climate

Hero-making superintendents are all about relationships of positive, unconditional regard at board meetings. Their *tasks* are done (paper shuffling), long before the board members arrive—even before the early ones arrive. Superintendents are not conferring with the assistant superintendent in the office, nor are they whispering with the school attorney at the end of the hall. They are also not arriving alongside board members; they are greeting board members, just as principals should be greeting teachers or students in each school every day.

Superintendents are ensuring that someone is asking board members if we can take their coats or get them anything. Hero makers might want to do this themselves. Superintendents also must pay particular attention to whom, and how often, they speak with board members, because if they do not stay mindful of this, they might unintentionally spend more time with their favorites.

It is a good rule of thumb to give each board member at least one positive affirmation. It helps the board maintain the energy to stay in a policymaking role. After all, those who feel good about themselves where they are (in policymaking and governance), need not go somewhere else to have their needs met negatively (micromanaging).

Hero-making superintendents should find every opportunity to ensure that board members are comfortable. Hero-making superintendents are "great contextualizers," offering confirmation of the value of board members' contributions, even when the contribution is more butt-headed than it is breathtaking. As noted previously, hero makers are the segues between the points made, the transitions between the paragraphs, and the grease for the machine. The climate that hero makers provide is one where people feel safe sharing what is on their mind, because what is on their mind usually has some value, even if mis-delivered during distress. More on distress is covered later in the book.

Basically, hero makers ensure that they are *all about relationships*, first, since it is only through positive relationships that tasks can be accomplished effectively.

Hero makers ensure that they are *all about relationships*, first, since it is only through positive relationships that tasks can be accomplished effectively.

Getting Down to Business

Hero makers will not let board members waste each other's time, nor that of the superintendent. Now you might think we're going to launch into a cheerleading chant for Roberts Rules of Order,* but we are really not. Roberts Rules of Order provide some structure for meetings that run the risk of becoming a bit more cumbersome in detailed discussion, but to be honest, if you have idiots running the meeting—especially without a hero maker in the room—Roberts Rules will not do much, except to create a dysfunctional conversation where someone really nasty competes to prove that he or she knows Roberts Rules better than the rest.

Point of order!!!!!

See what we mean?

> **Hero makers realize that the "how" of communication works much better than the "what."**

Hero makers realize that the "how" of communication works much better than the "what." We have found we can say just about anything to people (some things pretty far-reaching, indeed), when we are more mindful of the "how." It is not so much the words, although certain phrases do help, such as "Would it please the board if the administration team . . . ?" It is much more the nonverbals that allow us to get the business done most effectively.

Structures help as well. One that we recommend when allowed is a consent agenda, where items of smaller import (and ones that can take up a lot of meaningless banter if there are no guardrails around) can be acted on with one motion. Some of these are items of business that occur month after month, such as approving minutes from the previous meeting, or accepting certain written committee reports that come in regularly, or authorizing various expenditures when allowable through this method. It is not uncommon to see ten or more agenda items collapsed into one consent agenda action.

The beauty of a consent agenda is that board members receive these agendas ahead of time for review, and if board members feel that items need to be moved from the consent agenda to a regular agenda, they can make that request. It pays to share copies of all documents with board members ahead of time so that they can structure their thoughts and ready themselves for discussion. Paperwork should be well-organized and signposted, so that everything is in plain view for board members and easy to locate, and consistent in presentation from month-to-month.

Another tip for hero makers is to get a bit of business done—a healthy amount—before offering members of the community in attendance the time for input. Community input time is often when concerns are brought to the attention of the board, and this can be uncomfortable for board members (some love it, however). Either way, it runs the risk of taking people away from collaborative conversation, so anything you can do to maximize the number of productive conversations before a bit of contention enters the room is a good thing. That said, don't wait until midnight to have your community input, as that is probably a bit unfair, it brings out the crazies, and it will upset the board member whose aggrieved constituency is in the room.

A good strategy is to offer appropriately timed forums for community input, where people get only a few minutes per person to talk, up until a certain point. The point here is to put right-sized guardrails around this time: enough so the community feels it has been heard, but not too much so that things run the risk of going too long and detracting from the business that must get done.

Also, it always pays to schedule those times when the board must go behind closed doors ("executive session" to discuss disciplinary incidents with students, personnel issues with staff, items of attorney/client privilege, contract negotiations, etc.), near the end of the meeting, so that people are not left uncomfortably stewing in some waiting room or hallway together, or even before the public part of the meeting convenes. One benefit of having the executive session prior to the meeting is that it has an ending time, because we don't want to keep the public waiting. It can always reconvene later if needed.

The structure of board meetings, and how you conduct them, lends itself to good business practices and healthy discussions. Oh, and as we said at the beginning of this chapter—board meetings are meetings to conduct the business of the board. They're not

town hall meetings, where anyone who has the ability to repro-
duce has the ability to filibuster.

That said, hero makers clarify to the public—and in full view
of everyone—that although the board president may respond to
their concerns, he or she may only thank them for their comments
and contributions. Other board members are not obligated to
respond to folks who are angry with them (although some will
love the back-and-forth), and the board is not required to promise
that solutions will come their way for grievances aired.

Hero makers, of course, will offer the assurances that folks are
"heard," and that the leadership and administration will do whatever it can to look into [this or that] for the board, and will offer the
board president a report on what they find, as soon as it is doable.

Hero makers ensure that after the board meeting closes, board
members will drive home with the feeling that the evening spent
at school was well worth their time, talent, and contribution. They
feel great about their leadership and are proud of what they said,
and did, in the meeting.

They feel like heroes.

★ Hero-making Tips

◆ Hero makers ensure that every single thing done at a
board meeting is choreographed, to every extent possible, under their direction. Yet, at the same time, they do
not give that impression to others.

◆ Hero makers spend the weeks prior to board meetings
getting everything well-organized and disseminated to
their boards. They encourage a relationship with their
board so that if individual board members have concerns
they wish to express, they inform the board president
and superintendent prior to the meeting. The key to a
good relationship is that no "surprises" occur during the
meeting, even if disagreement is to take place or concerns
are to be aired.

- Hero makers ensure that they use "invisible time" productively prior to each board meeting. This is when they are in the boardroom by themselves prior to anyone else's arrival (except maybe their secretaries or the custodians), ensuring that the space is properly arranged, that seating is comfortable, that food and drink are available, and possibly even that soft music is playing so that no one arrives to an awkward silence.

- Hero makers are effective at making good recommendations for board action at board meetings. It helps to frame the issues constructively and gives board members the security to know that the actionable items have been vetted through the thinking process of the chief executive officer. It is a part of acting as a shield for board members. Board members are then welcome to move forward the recommendation through to board action, or to take a different path, but at least a professional recommendation is provided to the issues in front of them.

- Hero makers embrace their responsibility to make sure every word or action of their board is affirmed for its merit and contribution, even if it's not the way things are going to move forward.

- Hero makers are great storytellers and do so at board meetings without droning on or going for too long. Their purpose in storytelling is to ensure that those offering contributions can look backward with pride, and forward with hope. They serve as the deft contextualizers so that everyone's comment—even the thoughtless person's—has a bit of window dressing for public consumption.

- Hero makers ensure that they bring the *sizzle*, as well as the *steak*, to board meetings. So, before the board takes up any issue or motion, the superintendent has one or two options *that will work* (or at least will minimize collateral damage) so that the board doesn't appear to be out-of-options (and thus, appear to be unknowledgeable) in front of the public.

◆ Hero makers ensure that every good idea is someone else's, especially a board member's.

◆ Hero makers ensure that everything that goes right via board action is given to the board as credit, and everything that does not go right is embraced as the superintendent's responsibility. This is actually a part of their role as The Shield. The buck stops with the hero maker.

Note

* Remember the book by Henry Robert Martin that streamlines the parliamentary procedure of meetings—with motion, seconds, discussions, etc.? That's what we are referring to when we mentioned Roberts Rules of Order.

7

Between Board Meetings

How many of us have experienced the so-called big day, in whatever form it was, and then let our guard down for a few days (weeks or months) afterward? Examples might include the annual standardized testing window, the school accreditation visit, the final game of an athletic season, or even the final day of school in a given year.

"Whew!" We exhale.

Then, we take a much-needed rest.

Superintendents often feel this way after the big board meeting happening once or twice per month, and they especially feel it if they have working sessions between meetings, because these can be equally invigorating (taxing).

Hero makers know that only a brief exhale is wise.

For it is *between* board meetings that the seeds are sown for the most positive relations with board members. The hundreds of things that occur between board meetings

> **It is *between* board meetings that the seeds are sown for the most positive relations with board members.**

make board members heroes, or not, and as such, they must become the focus of our savviest superintendents.

We suggest a three-pronged approach to ensure that heroes are made, and maintained, between board meetings for the best of results:

First, superintendents must make a personal commitment to reach out and do something for each board member between meetings, something that wouldn't be in a superintendent's contract or job description.

Superintendents must intentionally be seen by each board member's constituency (key communicators) doing something that, in a positive manner, feeds the appetite (meets the needs) of each constituency.

Second, superintendents must intentionally be seen by each board member's constituency (key communicators) doing something that, in a positive manner, feeds the appetite (meets the needs) of each constituency.

Finally, superintendents must schedule some official, personal time with one board member per month, for a check-in and update on their perspective as to the superintendent's connection with the community. This is typically over breakfast, lunch, or dinner—or at the coffee shop.

Let us talk about the first item, a personal commitment to reach out and do something for each board member beyond what is in your job description. It might be to write a thank-you note to the board member's boss at work, who has provided the latitude for your board member to leave early once per month to attend the school board meetings. Noting their outstanding service, as any representative of their business would, is a nice touch. It could be to attend the funeral for a board member's extended family member, to offer condolences. It could be to show up at a community event that the board member is helping organize, to offer a bit of volunteer time—Toys for Tots, Highway Clean-Up, or Fill-the-Bus for the Soldiers. It might be to see the board member and family out at the ice cream shop after the big game or spelling bee, and offer not only your congratulations but also your thanks to the family for allowing mom or dad to help you run the school. These actions help in hero-making. The point is that hero makers become intentional about knowing what is important to board members, and what they are involved in, so that they specifically do something with unconditional positive regard that helps the board member to feel valued and important as a person.

The second is a bit more indirect, yet still intentional. Superintendents who know what board members value, know their constituencies. They also know where their constituencies spend their time. It is important that superintendents spend time there too, whether at the barbershop, the coffee shop, the private club, or the local delicatessen. Key in terms of hero-making is being seen having conversations with others, in a way that provides visible support and assistance for those causes that the constituencies champion.

If the conversation in the barber chair becomes one of voicing worry and support of the small business owner because of the impending arrival of the big-box, discount store, then it pays to have that conversation overheard. If it becomes one of praising the recent medical treatment and rehabilitation services at the local hospital's preventative care outlet (and the board member is in human resources at the hospital), then that might be a good move as well. If it becomes one of sharing the telephone number of a local politician who can help the farmers get crop subsidies if the draught gets any worse this season, that might be well worth getting overheard too. The point is not that you are inauthentic or calculatingly chameleon-like; instead, you are finding areas in which you can authentically be seen as being helpful to board members' constituencies when your values align, and then penciling-in opportunities to do just that.

The final point regarding the importance of between-board-meeting hero-making is to schedule a formal time, once a month, with one board member to have a candid conversation about how he or she perceives the school's business is doing, as well as your ability to connect with the

Schedule a formal time, once a month, with one board member to have a candid conversation about how he or she perceives the school's business is doing.

community. Then, remember what is said and work to address

any concerns the member might have. The school credit card should not pay for these meals, of course; it is sort of the equivalent of what we all used to do in terms of stocking our classrooms with the necessary supplies to teach—we use our own money. Same here. You're investing by stocking your personal toolkit with knowledge that will help you lead—and hero-make. These meetings, no more than an hour or two of your time (at your board member's convenience), will allow you to get at the heart of whether or not you are being a hero maker. If you find that you are connecting with the community after a "real" conversation, then we assure you that your board member is someone's hero who is important to him or her.

If not, you have some more work to do.

One question we hear from time to time is this: I cannot even get my board member to talk to me, let alone go out for a meal with me. What am I to do? In this instance, either this person is just in need of a major chill pill, or the situation has deteriorated to a point where many more deposits will need to be made in the relationship, before any withdrawals in terms of communication or candor could be expected. We suggest you simply then choose someone in your school district whom you trust, or someone in the community close to that board member, to have the same type of conversation to garner input. If you follow through, word will get back to your board member of the overture, and your attentiveness.

Hero makers minimize the "exhale" that happens after the big meeting, and then consider each next day's best work as directly proportional to the next meeting's success.

The main point to remember here is that hero makers minimize the "exhale" that happens after the big meeting, and then consider each next day's best work as directly proportional to the next meeting's success.

If board members feel valued on a consistent basis, they are less likely to need the spotlight of a board meeting to feel important. By nurturing the relationships with board members and appropriately stroking egos between board meetings, you can diminish their needs to feel important when the lights are shining and the news reporters are taking notes at the next public meeting.

Never lose sight of the power of a well-placed compliment. Every time someone receives a compliment, he or she thinks the person giving it is just a little smarter. It needs to be sincere, but it can be quite specific.

Never lose sight of the power of a well-placed compliment. Every time someone receives a compliment, he or she thinks the person giving it is just a little smarter.

We always need to look for the good things in others, even if we need to squint.

⊗ Hero-making Tips

♦ Hero makers realize that what happens between board meetings is at times even more critical than what happens *at* board meetings. Each board member brings to each meeting the cumulative emotions that have been acquired since the last meeting, whether positive or negative. Hero makers are on a continual quest for emotion management.

♦ Hero makers realize that they can tell their board members what they stand for all they want, but this won't do much good. Board members need to have hero makers *show* them what they stand for, and if this is through the whisper of someone to whom the board member is connected and respects, all the better.

♦ Hero makers remember that if board members resist their overtures to have conversations or spend time with them once or twice per year, they must be forgiven in advance because the refusal is indicative of a future teachable moment, when the hero maker can make a difference in this person's life.

8

Advancing by Retreating

The last couple of chapters have talked about working with the school board on a regular basis—during regularly scheduled meetings and in between. Obviously these times are essential. However, there are also special events that are important. One of these special situations is when we have the chance to make great strides in terms of board relationships and knowledge. We must take advantage of these rare opportunities.

In our work with superintendents, boards, and school districts, we have many times noticed the value of time spent when the entire governance team comes together outside of the regular board meeting schedule. This has especially been true when we facilitated school board retreats. Here are some observations we have made over the years:

Hero makers who facilitate the professional development of their boards through annual retreats provide two things that are very important: (1) an opportunity for board members to see and feel the experience of being a student of leadership and governance, while stepping away from their familiar boardroom dynamic, and (2) an opportunity for board members to get to know each other better personally, and to get to know their hero makers better as well.

Retreats can and do come in all shapes, sizes, and formats, and while we are not necessarily going to recommend one flavor or other, we will stress the need to have all board members participate, if at all possible. In fact, having this as an expectation that the board president shares with members while they are candidates for election is important in that if the entire board does not commit to new learning together, each year, then they will have a much more difficult time making a positive difference through the responsibili-

> If the entire board does not commit to new learning together, each year, then they will have a much more difficult time making a positive difference through the responsibilities they embrace.

ties they embrace. Boards need to stay current, and they must do this together.

We recommend the following actions when planning for an annual retreat:

Location

Lost Arrow Resort in the State of Michigan uses a slogan, "The Closest Place to Far Away!". It is a great place, with a small conference building, cabins and rooms of various sizes, a restaurant, river cruises, a petting zoo, and trails to walk. It seems to have something for everyone: public spaces, private spaces, and everything in-between.

What is particularly noteworthy about its location is that it really *is* the closest place to far away. The typical drive to Lost Arrow is not too long for most who travel there, yet when you arrive, it really does seem like you are far away from home.

It just gives that "feel" when you drive onto the expansive property.

We're not suggesting you take your board to Lost Arrow (although it would be very nice); we are suggesting that whatever destination you select allows board members to feel as though they are "getting away" while they are with you—to their own "closest place to far away."

For optimal learning to occur, you and your board must be able to be wherever you are, in the moment, and feeling a bit special about being there as well. Yet, in the back of all of your minds and with the busy daily lives we all lead, when it is getting time to go back home, you do not want a long trip on their minds. You do, however, want board members to take enough of a drive—separately or in groups—to be able to process what has been learned and experienced. You will want to be glad that they stepped away and feel like it was some time well-earned by their service.

You will also want to ensure that whatever location you select, the people working at that location know who is coming from your board and why, and will work overboard to ensure your board feels special and important being there. Provide a photograph of your board with their names to the facility manager, and ask that their staff use board member names whenever possible (*Mr. So-&-So, Ms. So-&-So, Dr. So-&-So,* etc.).

Every detail that you can personalize or individualize in terms of comfort for your board . . . "Do it." This is particularly important in terms of environmental preferences. Some members prefer working and learning in groups, while others prefer to work and learn alone. Since the retreat will primarily be about group learning, you should ensure that time is also provided for board members to take a stroll, to get some alone time if they wish, and even to make a telephone call or two, if they need to intermittently plug-in, in order to unplug.

Itinerary

We strongly recommend that hero makers consider the following method to divide up time spent at an annual retreat: (1) board of education group goals and a focus on board business and school governance for the coming year; (2) training and professional development in stewardship, leadership, and governance, and (3) the superintendent's goals that the board will oversee.

Board Goals

Goals and a focus on board business and school governance are recommended in terms of a board's own vision and mission. The vision is where the board ideally would like to arrive regarding its own work and governance at the end of a time period (one year, three years, five years); the mission is what they will focus on as they are attempting to get there (how they will behave, what they will discuss). It's important to discuss and clarify these goals because this is where hero makers are able to validate someone's pet project (or pet peeve) through transparent discussion, prioritization, and hopefully consensus. Whether or not the hero maker facilitates this discussion is really best left to the local dynamic and the preferences of the board and board president.

Often, an outside facilitator is able to say things to the board that the superintendent is not, regarding how and under what conditions they might reach consensus on the more challenging issues. The crux of the matter here is that the board discusses what their priorities are for the upcoming year, and why, over time, hero makers are able to help their boards understand that individual members who allowed their goals to take a second seat in years past may need a bit more consideration this time, as they have deferred patiently while others have taken precedence. That is, if they are good ideas.

Professional Development

Training and professional development are necessary for boards to remain current with the issues that the school district is facing, and they also allow board members to showcase themselves as lead learners to teachers, students, and families. This is a great place for superintendents to provide a legislative and legal update, as well as those items that may be new in terms of the state department of education. It is critical that a hero maker never refers to "the state" as the bad guy, or gives any impression that the local school district is being victimized by some new law, edict, or policy.

Hero makers remain above the fray and do not whine.

Hero makers demonstrate to boards that although challenges come the way of local schools, *your* superintendent will remain in touch with policy makers and will continually put forth effort in educating them about the needs of your school district, and will showcase the phenomenal work that the teachers, students, and families are doing.

The *consummate contextualizer* in each of us as a hero maker always turns challenge into opportunity, and hero makers have information on how the board's work will be critical and incredibly important as we navigate what lies ahead in the school year. And hero makers always remain positive. This is the piece where hero makers demonstrate good stewardship, as our best caretakers continually encourage those in their care to *Don't worry, be happy.*

Hero makers continually offer the impression, "Everything will be okay, as we have the A-team on the issue and the greatest community on earth."

Hero makers continually offer the impression, "Everything will be okay, as we have the A-team on the issue and the greatest community on earth."

At some point in the training and professional development portion of the day, the hero maker must step away from the podium and become a co-learner with the board. This is where everyone goes to school and learns something new.

The subject of leadership always has a derivative that could be delivered through a great presenter in an hour or two of time. It will be key for the hero maker to help with the lesson planning beforehand. There must be some goal or objective that the hero maker wants the board to learn—whether it is about relationships with one another, about the board's policymaking roles (without micromanagement), or about consensus building and conflict resolution. The new learning could be about community stewardship, about dealing with difficult people in the grocery store, or about work-life balance and how leaders must be comfortable

Our best hero makers use another's voice to reinforce a point that they want made to their board, so that their board becomes more like the kind of policymaking body that the hero maker desires.

with imbalance. It could be about a myriad of topics.

Our best hero makers use another's voice to reinforce a point that they want made to their board, so that their board becomes more like the kind of policymaking body that the hero maker desires.

Superintendent Goals

Using the retreat as an opportunity to have an initial discussion of the goals that the board has for the superintendent is also an annual necessity. The board president or another board member could facilitate this section of the retreat. An hour or so could be used for this purpose, as the aim is not to finalize the goals at this juncture, but rather to talk about some possibilities and why they are important. This really is not an evaluation of the superintendent by any means; that would not be a good place for it. Rather, it may include having the superintendent reflect on some of the expectations that the board had of the superintendent the year prior, and what was done with them.

Hero makers use these discussions as an opportunity to plant seeds in the board members' minds regarding what they feel would be important, yet they do so in a way that gives the board the impression that it was their idea. *"When I was talking with our board treasurer, Bob, recently, and got the impression that although last year was a great year in terms of adding to our fund equity, we all may benefit if I am more intentional in messaging locally how we are managing our finances. We almost have enough for a new stadium. I'm always open to any ideas you have, in terms of my goals, and I appreciated that being brought up, as I might not have thought as directly about it otherwise."*

Takeaways

Effectively scheduled and delivered, a hero maker's retreat allows the board to see itself as responsible for doing something besides being in charge of the school district. It provides a collective awareness that as a body, the members have the responsibility *to themselves* and others to remain headed in a direction that they collectively agree is important. This reduces ambiguity, uncertainty, and hopefully kneejerk reactions to the squeaky wheels that will always present themselves with agendas that may fall left or right of the direction the board wishes to go.

Effectively scheduled and delivered, a hero maker's retreat allows the board to see itself as responsible for doing something besides being in charge of the school district.

The annual retreat provides an opportunity for the board members to grow and develop in their professional knowledge and leadership abilities, and as we have discussed, with an enhanced skill set of any kind, self-efficacy develops, in which one's increased confidence and self-concept increases the possibility that needs will be met positively, as opposed to negatively. And it provides the opportunity for the hero maker to share his or her appreciation for and willingness to embrace the goals the board has set, while also providing assurances that if the board allows the superintendent as Chief Operating Officer to operationalize policy, it will be done with the board's authority and governance desires in mind. It may reduce micromanagement.

Finally, a hero maker's retreat provides a great opportunity for hero makers to treat board members like heroes—through location, service, and itinerary. People coming together with other people can enhance everyone's desire to work as a team and appreciate the time, talent, and treasures everyone brings to this leadership opportunity.

In short, hero makers assist their boards in advancing by retreating.

⭐ Hero-making Tips

◆ Hero makers ensure that the care and feeding that they provide board members between meetings is amplified by staff members working at the location of the annual retreat. They proactively contact location managers and share that this is what they expect in paying for the use of their facilities. And, they have a contact on site who will crack the whip behind the scenes, if the superintendent whispers in his or her ear.

◆ Hero makers ensure that they provide board members options regarding the board's goals, as well as the superintendent's. This is not done so much to predetermine how the board will decide upon what to focus; rather, it is done so that the board will not have to think too hard while at the event. Board members can always offer additional goals at their pleasure, and these may be better and more palatable if they do not have to think too hard in the process.

◆ Hero makers offer ideas (plant seeds) a year in advance when they want something important from their board, such as extensions of their own contract timelines or additional benefits in their compensation packages. This way, the board has time to mull it over, and does not feel rushed or blindsided in the retreat setting.

◆ Hero makers refer back to the learning of the retreats at future meetings, so as to deepen the understanding of all board members regarding the time well-spent and the important topics of study.

9

Board Personalities: The "I" in Team

Many of us have heard the saying, "There is no 'I' in team," meaning with a play on words that as the letter *I* is literally not in the spelling of the word "team," so in our teamwork, we should refrain from thinking only about ourselves.

In the context of boards of education, this message would seem to say to board members, "Put aside your individual preferences for the greater good of the board and school system."

In a sense, this seems fitting with the message of our book, yet ironically, if hero makers want this to happen, they actually start by doing the opposite—paying attention to the I's." This is because every single board of education no matter the quality is made up of somewhere between five and nine I's."

Every board member is *first* an I, at the subconscious level, with unique layers of individuality influencing how he or she behaves and works with others.

This is actually a great opportunity for us, as understanding the I is key to knowing how to bring people together through better decision making in support of what the superintendent wants to do. It starts with a focus on individual board members, not simply on what everyone accomplishes together.

he trick is not to consider first and foremost where the group is headed, but rather *why* each individual is either contributing or not contributing to the group's direction, as the hero maker would intend it.

Why they are doing it for themselves.

In leadership development, we pose at times that it really should be all about the adults in the schools *first*, if we want things to be all about the children *most*. It is really no different here, where it is all about each individual board member first, if we want it to be all about the entire board *most*.

It is all about each individual board member first, if we want it to be all about the entire board *most*.

What follows is an explanation grounded in years of practical psychology resting upon one of the most comprehensive theoretical bases known worldwide, which we will share later in the book.

People are complicated.

We have learned from Dr. Nate Regier, co-author of *Beyond Drama: Transcending Energy Vampires*, who has an impressive background in psychology and consulting, that factors of our physiology and personality can be conceived as making up the core of who we are. We believe that our physical and cognitive capabilities have a relationship with what we can accomplish, and our personalities help influence this potential.

We see this in our board members, don't we?

These characteristics are more deeply rooted and do not change rapidly.

In addition, Dr. Regier notes that we all have factors of circumstances in our lives that we have to deal with on a daily basis. We believe that this is the luggage that either assists or resists our boundaries of performance. Board members bring luggage with them to the board as well. These could be whether or not we are rich or poor, or whether or not we are superintendent of a struggling school district or of one that is achieving.

Luggage can be switched out more easily in some cases and less easily in others. It influences how we travel.

Dr. Regier also notes how something else helps us to navigate the circumstances we face: our factors of identity. One of these, self-efficacy, is particularly influential. We have all seen those on our board who have a healthy sense of self-efficacy and others who do not.

It continues to amaze us how well-adjusted some of our board members are, despite personal challenge or professional circumstance, and how others pop a sprocket when the littlest of things happens. Certainly, having healthy self-efficacy better allows our board members to use their personalities to navigate the demands of circumstance thrust upon them, and our school districts.

> Having healthy self-efficacy better allows our board members to use their personalities to navigate the demands of circumstance thrust upon them, and our school districts.

All of this is happening, month by month, inside each of the I's in your team—in each board member, of course.

All of these very personal and individually complicated variables are in play, inside each board member, as board meetings are occurring and group decisions are being made. Five to nine people have their insides trying to interact with their outsides, and their senses of individual "self" and "self-competence" are either helping or hampering.

Focusing solely on the group and/or ignoring this inside awkwardness that each board member experiences would be ignoring one dangerous blind spot, said another way, a big elephant in the room.

One difficulty that some superintendents have with their boards is that they run around trying to adjust (or hide) present circumstance to form better relationships, but they don't typically learn how to work on their board members' insides, to get optimal performance, despite the luggage carried.

We have found the secret to what hero makers can do about this. Later in the book, we get into some practical strategies for dealing with personalities, and our extended-length Special Feature goes much further for those interested in the theory and psychological approaches that will help superintendents with their boards, and everyone else for that matter. Before moving forward, let us share a bit more information about the theory that will be covered in our Special Feature: Board Personalities and the Process Communication Model.

Approximately 40 years of developing theory derived from the field of clinical psychology provides a formula of how personality can be understood so that people can better connect with one other. Now this is not your typical personality-type indicator, with clever qualifiers, memorable acronyms, or even a free, downloadable report. It is not a pamphlet or website that says we're a "this type" or "that type," and it certainly does not claim that by virtue of our type, we are either better suited to leadership or board service, or not.

It is something much different, deeply theoretical and yet practical.

In studying this model, we have encouraged more than 100 Ph.D. students in recent years to find a more comprehensive, descriptive, and predictive framework for human behavioral analysis, and to date, they have not been able to provide us a better model.

And these are some sharp people on the search.

Please know that as we share this model in *The Hero Maker*, we as authors make no claim of ownership or originality in describing the model, and we are grateful to those mentioned in these sections, for their willingness to let us include their work inside our own, as well as references to their works. If you choose to read and learn more, you will assuredly be able to very much understand the complexities of board member personalities, especially when they are the most complicated of puzzles.

⭑ Hero-making Tips

◆ Hero makers operate each and every day to consider the needs of adults first, so that we can all be about the children *most*. They understand that in the event of cabin depressurization, oxygen masks go on the adults first, so that they can help others with theirs.

- Hero makers understand that each team member has an inescapable *I* that must receive the proper care and feeding, before the team can function. They debunk the adage, "There is no 'I' in team," and actively teach their district and building leaders to do the same.
- Hero makers understand the importance of building and encouraging self-efficacy in their board members, because once board members have a positive belief that through hard work and earned effort they can make a difference, they are more apt to take on hard work (board-level responsibilities) and put forth an earned effort not to micromanage.
- Hero makers understand that from time to time, it is important to study something a bit more academic and not as easy-to-digest, for with patience in comprehension and application, it may provide some longer-term answers that will amplify one's influence on the board.

Reference

Regier, N., & King, J. (2013). *Beyond Drama: Transcending Energy Vampires*. Newton, KS: Next Element Publishing.

10

Board Personalities: Doors and the Dance of Drama

In the book *The Secret Solution: How One Principal Discovered the Path to Success* (Whitaker, Miller, & Donlan, 2013), some of the typical personalities that we find employed in K-12 school buildings are depicted through parable. It is the story of Principal Roger Rookie at Anytown Middle School, with three groups of teachers: the Superstars, the Fence-Sitters, and the Bullies. Characters such as Sandy Starr, Edgar Sleeper, and Carl Chameleon are among the starring roles. Those who read the book tell us they really do have these characters working in their schools.

The archetypes are everywhere. We see typical archetypes on boards of education as well.

Over the years, we have met Hank Hillbilly, Gabby Gossip, and Simon Suit. We often see Al Athletic and Braxton Bean Counter. Marge Micro gets elected after a superintendent spends too much money, and Yogi Union joins the board when teachers are upset.

What hero makers know about these roles is that while appearing rather predictable on the surface, something lies deeper within their personalities that influences what they say, what they do, and what they need.

Do you ever wonder why some conversations with board members are easy to have, and others feel like a tooth extraction? Similarly, isn't it true that with some board members, you find that conversations lead to where you intended, and with others, the discussions often seem to take a wrong turn, even though you painstakingly prepared? With some conversations you feel better after having had them than you did going in, and with others, the opposite. Because of these circumstances, you might over time avoid having conversations with some of your board members, and they with you.

That is not at all productive.

Consider a metaphor regarding "doors" and our communication preferences (Kahler, 1996, 2015; Kahler, 2008, with credit to the discoveries and work of Dr. Paul Ware as well). We all have a door that is our favorite door, and every time someone knocks on it, we hear the person, and we open it wide. We also have another door that is nailed shut, and we don't even hear when someone knocks. In our other doors, we can only hear the knocks part of the time. Communication occurs optimally through open doors (Kahler, 1996, 2015; Kahler, 2008).

We have these doors, and so do our board members. They exist in our personalities.

Are we all opening our doors completely through an understanding of each other's personalities, so that no misunderstandings take place?

The personalities of our board members provide us clues as to which doors to use. How we open those doors is often as important as what we say, once we do. What is so interesting about using open doors with each other is that if we do so, the positive aspects of our personality tend to shine, and relationships thrive.

Consider the many things our personalities provide for us as noted by Kahler (2008). Our personalities provide us with the preferred perceptions in how we view the world (thinking, feeling, etc.). They provide us with preferred communication and management styles, in terms of how we want others to relate to us (Kahler, 2008). Our personalities give us environmental preferences in how we want our workspaces arranged, and whether we want to work together in groups, in pairs, or alone (Kahler, 2008).

They provide us with our primary motivation for doing what we do, which often has to do with being someone's hero, of course (more on this later), and our personalities even provide us with certain psychological needs that if met, give us the energy to work with other people, even those very different from us (Kahler, 2008).

Yet, personalities provide something else as well. While it is true that our personalities bring many positives to our leadership and service, it is also true that our personalities bring with them certain blind spots, causing us at times to come across to others in a way that we cannot see.

Board members are no exception, and we recall from previous chapters that it is a hero maker's job to function as a shield to those board members who are unaware of how they are coming across. Hero makers can use their knowledge of personality to protect their board members from the unanticipated consequences of their blind spots.

> **Hero makers can use their knowledge of personality to protect their board members from the unanticipated consequences of their blind spots.**

Consider the overly persistent questioning from a board member that could result in your best local contractor pulling a great bid that will provide the safest playground equipment. Consider the insensitivity perceived in a board member that could tip the scales of a parent filing a frivolous lawsuit. Consider the board member who frequently seems to focus on what is wrong, rather than what is good about something.

Over time, what is the effect?

Public dissatisfaction, of course. Employee discontent as well.

Hero makers who study personality provide both "saves" and "assists" to board members for better outcomes.

We all have experienced conversations at board meetings in which board members can become critical, suspicious, defiant, manipulative, mistake-prone, or timid (Donlan, 2015). What is fascinating is that these behaviors are predictable, and even avoidable. When board members behave as such, this is an advertisement that

..ero maker's attention is needed, and that attention is needed with knowledge and an understanding of one's *personality*.

Without such attention, we will see drama escalate in which all involved can play the roles of perpetrators, victims, and rescuers (Karpman, 2014).

A drama triangle (Karpman, 2014)!

Have we ever had drama at board meetings?

What is fascinating (yet worrisome) is that those involved in drama perform a predictable dance, and it is at times a more natural feeling to join the dance than to decline the invitation.

In the dance of the drama triangle (Karpman, 1968; Karpman, 2014; Regier & King, 2013), persecutors often seek out victims, and victims tend to oblige them. Victims look for rescuers, and rescuers are drawn to them. Rescuers keep a watch for persecutors as well, and when they find them, they will find victims to save.

It's a true relationship of co-dependency.

Consider the community member with a mousy look on her face and a whiny sound in her voice (potentially rehearsed, but possibly not even with her awareness), reporting to the board that her child is getting picked on by your "nasty high school assistant principal." Singled-out, of course! Envision the board member helicoptering in and mentioning to the parent that the board will "take care of that."

The dance is on, starring: the Victimized Parent (and child), and in absentia, the Prosecutorial Assistant Principal and, of course, at 500 feet descending with harness dangling . . . the Rescuing Board Member.

Drama provides first a curtsy, then a full-blown embrace, as it begins to move around the triangle, yet hero makers can stop it before the dance starts. They recognize when the music is about to begin and with an understanding of personality, can circumvent it.

If any of this is recognizable to you, or if learning about what you can do when you see the drama triangle unfold at your own board meeting piques your interest, you might spend time reading our Special Feature that goes into more detail about these personalities and what is happening psychologically with miscommunication. Our feature also includes information on how hero makers can connect with board members of differing personality types to make a positive difference in communication, while minimizing drama's dance and the roles that are a result.

It is a deep dive if you're interested.

One takeaway regarding board personalities is that we cannot really change the hardwiring of others, so we might as well learn to connect with it. Doing so will bring out the best in board members' personalities, as hero makers know where to provide open doors of communication.

> **One takeaway regarding board personalities is that we cannot really change the hardwiring of others, so we might as well learn to connect with it.**

As we began our chapter, we envisioned the archetype board personalities of Hank Hillbilly, Gabby Gossip, and Simon Suit. Looking at their unique individualities is what personality analysis allows us, as it might reveal that Al Athletic and Braxton Bean Counter can focus their positive energy on other things besides sports and our fund balance. We might not be able to stop Marge Micro from requesting itemized receipts from the elementary candy sales, or Yogi Union from holding court in his weekly coffee klatch, yet we can make inroads to better conversations through consideration of this short story that began over 40 years ago, one that has inspired personality analysis worldwide.

In the late 1960s, while working as a clinical intern in a mental health treatment center, Taibi Kahler began making some innovative psychological discoveries. One theory earned him the Eric Berne Memorial Scientific Award from the International Transactional Analysis Association for the most impressive scientific discovery of the year (Kahler, 2008). Because this award was conferred with the support of 10,000 of Taibi's colleagues in 52 countries, his work attracted worldwide attention.

A few years later, the National Aeronautic Space Administration's (NASA) leading psychiatrist for manned spaceflight, Dr. Terry McGuire, was working to enhance the American Space Program's astronaut selection processes. In learning of Taibi Kahler's work, he found that specific theory could predict how astronauts would work with others in handling the rigors of spaceflight (Kahler, 2008).

Through further research and work with NASA, Dr. Kahler refined his developing models of personality and communication, finding applications in the corporate, therapeutic, and governmental sectors. During the years following, Dr. Kahler expanded his model's applications to non-profit service, health care, spiritual applications, and education.

In the early 1990s, the United States National Democratic Committee asked Dr. Kahler to serve as a psycho-demographer in the presidential campaign of William Jefferson Clinton. President Clinton also received training in the model (Kahler, 2008). The Process Communication Model® (PCM) is now used worldwide to offer a positive difference in people's lives and includes K-12 educational applications in the Process Education Model® (PEM) in terms of leading, teaching, and learning.

We think PCM can help hero makers to encourage positive relations and productivity in your board members as well. Of course, you are the best judge of whether or not PCM would be valuable to you in your superintendency. For an extended read on how all of this personality information fits together, please consider visiting our Special Feature at the end of this book. While a more academic read, it could be powerful for hero makers in learning more about their board members' personalities, and their own.

⭐ Hero-making Tips

◆ Hero makers find the pearls in board member personalities to forge a connection and recognize how to nurture that to a new level of closeness and mutual respect. That hillbilly on our board might be a member of Mensa International.

◆ Hero makers first strive to understand their own personalities and especially their own blind spots, to determine how they might behave while under pressure and to have the capacity to connect with people very different from them.

◆ Hero makers realize that when people around them are in the dance of drama, it is more difficult to resist joining the dance than to accept the invitation. Staying out of drama takes practice, patience, and persistence.

◆ Hero makers understand that if they must ask board members to stretch the capabilities of the talents they bring to the board, then they must first focus on where people are naturally strong. It is like exercising the good leg to rehabilitate the other.

References

Donlan, R. (2015, January). The Power of "Process" for Superintendents. *New Superintendents E-Journal.* Alexandria, VA: American Association of School Administrators.

Kahler, T. (1996, 2015). *The Process Communication Model® Seminar: Seminar One/Core Topics.* Hot Springs, AR: Kahler Communications, Inc.

Kahler, T. (2008). *The Process Therapy Model: The Six Personality Types with Adaptations.* Little Rock, AR: Taibi Kahler Associates, Inc.

Karpman, S. B. (1968). Fairy Tales and Script Drama Analysis. *Transactional Analysis Bulletin 26* (7), 39–43.

Karpman, S. B. (2014). *A Game-Free Life: The Definitive Book on the Drama Triangle and the Compassion Triangle by the Originator and Author.* San Francisco, CA: Drama Triangle Publications.

Regier, N., & King, J. (2013). *Beyond Drama: Transcending Energy Vampires.* Newton, KS: Next Element Publishing.

Whitaker, T., Miller, S., & Donlan, R. (2013). *The Secret Solution: How One Principal Discovered the Path to Success.* Lanham, MD: Rowman & Littlefield Education.

11

Starting Undefeated

Education is such an unusual profession. There are clear starting points—the first day of school and other equally well-defined finish lines—the final day of school, graduation, etc. Typically, most new faculty members start their jobs on a certain date in a predetermined month which allows for some consistency in establishing expectations for the group. These situations allow for natural changes and growth. If we add 20 or 2,000 new employees all at once, we bring in a potential jolt of new ideas and energy. The enthusiasm level starts high, and the energy is palpable. This is a chance to bring about significant change.

Principals can establish differing expectations for teachers and students than were in place the previous year. Teachers can tweak the way they arrange the furniture, handle their classroom management practices, or refine their instruction. Each year, this is a prime time to alter or grow the climate or even the culture of a school.

This same opportunity arises for the superintendent.

The beginning of the year is a special time. Many districts have opening sessions where all employees get together and the excitement can be felt in the auditorium. Other professions are not afforded this opportunity. Imagine how difficult it is to build enthusiasm in a regular business office where every day feels the same. May is like November; Tuesday is like Friday.

You may have hired 50 new employees over the last year, but basically it was one a week, and they quickly become indoctrinated into the way things are typically done and have been done for years. Schools are not like this.

A district leader has a chance to reestablish expectations and relationships on an annual or even perennial basis.

A district leader has a chance to reestablish expectations and relationships on an annual or even perennial basis. Although certain things may have occurred that make it more challenging, the start of the year provides that new hope. This same opportunity can be there for board relations. There are elections, new officers, and the beginning of a school year that can allow for changes in practices. However, the best chance we will have as hero makers is when we first start in the role. This is especially true if when we start as superintendent, we are also new to the district.

The First Day of School

We often hear that teachers have to earn students' respect, but actually that is not true. Students usually behave very well the first day of school. Teachers are given that gift. Now what they do with it is up to them.

This same thing applies to principals. When they are first appointed, the teachers dress better, and everyone is actually on time for the first meeting. What the principal does from that point forward determines if there will be a new norm, or if some teachers will quickly revert to arriving late for meetings and dressing more unprofessionally than we might wish. The principal had that window, as brief as might have been, to alter the school quickly and effectively.

Superintendents are also given that gift. Often when we are first hired, board members are on their finest behavior. They are doing their thing with politeness so that they can impress their new hire and make sure they get on his or her good side. This is an incredible opportunity for superintendents that they may not have again. This group came together and chose *you*. They want you to help them lead the school district. You were their choice. Now is the time to establish roles with the group.

If you did this during the interview, that is very powerful, but we still need to make sure these things are established while we are all still smiling. This is never done in a directive or offensive way, of course. Many examples of how to word things, what language to use, etc., have been shared in previous chapters. But if we miss this window, it may never reopen. We are helping our board members to be heroes by teaching them how to function and interact with the public, with each other, and with you.

Think of it as the first day on the job.

When you first walk into the office, the secretary wants to know how you want her to answer the phone. She wants to please the new boss. However, she only wants to know how to answer the phone up until the point when she actually answers the phone. Then she doesn't want to know how to answer the phone. Because at this point you are correcting her behavior; you are no longer establishing expectations.

This is exactly the same dynamic with your board.

They chose you. They want you to succeed.

Now is the best opportunity to help provide guidance for them on how to best make that happen. If it doesn't happen now, when will it?

A similar opportunity is available with new board members. Meeting with candidates before the election can be a great time to help build a relationship, and it can also be a time to help them understand how to be most effective in their potential new role. Meeting with all candidates is key, in order not to show preference. Neutrality is key! Obviously once the new candidates are elected or appointed, it becomes imperative to help provide them the guidance you both need to be successful. If there is a board president or individual member who can assist with this, that may be beneficial, but it is critical that you work to make sure the relationship starts off on as productive of a note as possible. You might also meet with those who were not elected, to thank them for their desire to serve.

Our roles are so complex that we can never stay undefeated in the eyes of everyone for very long. But regardless, we have to do what is right. That is the only thing that always works out in the long run.

Our roles are so complex that we can never stay undefeated in the eyes of everyone for very long. But regardless, we have to do what is right. That is the only thing that always works out in the long run.

It would be nice if the community agrees with every decision we make. It would be wonderful if the school board agrees with every decision we make. It is essential that we agree with every decision we make.

⭐ Hero-making Tips

◆ Hero makers realize that their first "at-bat" is their only *first* at-bat. They still have the opportunity to make home runs for the rest of their career, but they will not again have an opportunity to make a home run on their first at-bat.

◆ Hero makers realize that their leadership has a grade-point average, just like students have grade-point averages in school. They know that their earlier grades from board members will have much more of an impact on their leadership tenure grade, because they weigh-in more significantly. And even though board members tend to focus on the here and how, those things that superintendents do later on will have not as big of an impact on their overall job-performance grade, as they try to catch up.

◆ Hero makers realize that at the end of a day, week, semester, or school year, they will not remain completely undefeated, so it is important to have had honor in the way they played the game of their leadership. After all, each and every person inducted into any given sports hall of fame had a win/loss record that included some losses. Those are what define our greatest hero makers. Failing forward is part of the "All Other Duties as Assigned."

12

The Tour of Duty

Is there an optimal length of a superintendent's tour of duty in one location? Donlan and Gruenert (2016) asked this when they envisioned an actuarial table for leadership, in terms of dog years, in their book *Minds Unleashed: How Principals Can Lead the Right-Brained Way*.

Using the helpful information as the authors did from dog years.com, we offer the following:

TABLE 12.1 Comparison of Dog Years to Human Years

Dog Years	Human Years
1 year old	15 years old
2 years old	24 years old
3 years old	28 years old
4 years old	32 years old
5 years old	37 years old
6 years old	42 years old
7 years old	47 years old
8 years old	52 years old
9 years old	57 years old
10 years old	62 years old

Source: Information provided at www.dogyears.com.

The authors offered some metaphorical parallels that we'll extend-on here in terms of hero making (Donlan & Gruenert, 2016).

In leadership's first year, does one have the hero making maturity of a 15-year-old (Donlan & Gruenert, 2016), thinking one knows all the answers? The authors mention both insecurity and overconfidence, which could impede hero making without mentorship.

In leadership's third year, does one have the hero making maturity of a 28-year-old (Donlan & Gruenert, 2016)? The authors mentioned knowing what one wants at this age, which we believe is a hero making asset.

In leadership's fifth year, does one have the hero making maturity of a 37-year-old (Donlan & Gruenert, 2016)? We feel these are primetime opportunities for hero making, as the district starts to embody the values of a superintendent.

In leadership's tenth year, does one have the hero making maturity of a 62-year-old (Donlan & Gruenert, 2016)? The authors mention wisdom, which can be employed judiciously in the creation of heroes.

Is there a time when it is simply best that superintendents move to another location, so that they can put some more vim and vigor into their leadership?

We would like to ask the following: Is there a time when it is simply best that superintendents move to another location, so that they can put some more vim and vigor into their leadership? Of course, we realize that some simply move because of other circumstances, such as the desire for a new challenge or to live in another locale with family.

With that acknowledged, should hero makers from time to time have a "re-do" on their hero-making?

Does the superintendency have an optimal tour-of-duty lifespan?

Consider what a tour of duty involves.

In an ideal tour of duty in leadership and governance of a school district, everyone would know their roles and a well-oiled machine would be charting a course for educational excellence with almost military precision. Boards would be setting policy, establishing budget, evaluating the hero makers from time to time, but most of all, getting out of the way of daily operations.

Superintendents would be doing their part as well, leading the business of schools, finding the best talent to deploy, then managing, teaching, and supporting those at the building level, and most important, tending to the relationships between themselves and their boards, so that this fine chorus of activity moves forward, uninterrupted.

In terms of an optimal tour of duty, we will now discuss what might happen between the superintendent and board on an annual basis, so that one school season builds on the last, and moves effortlessly into the next. We want all in an educational community to experience continuous improvement in which a superintendent's tenure is one in which there's only one driver in the driver's seat—the hero maker.

An optimal tour of duty involves the superintendent serving in seven key roles as any given year progresses: (1) Superintendent as Concierge; (2) Superintendent as Lead Learner; (3) Superintendent as Vision-Gatherer; (4) Superintendent as Consensus-Builder; (5) Superintendent as Quality-Assurance Provider, (6) Superintendent as Steward; (7) Superintendent as Responsibility-Taker; and (8) Superintendent as Meaning-Maker.

Superintendent as Concierge welcomes new members to the board, provides them information on how to make their stay as comfortable as possible, offers directions to anything that might bolster sustenance and nourishment, and generally offers an ever-attentive presence where "Nothing is a problem, as asked," and "No question is too big or too small." Key to this role is that hero makers strive to offer more positive attention to the new board members, upon arrival, than the negative faction will. Consider what happens in schools when the new students enroll. The most welcoming fellow students are often the ones who lead them astray. The same happens with new teachers. Note how inviting toxic staff members are, as they are recruiting for their ranks. New board members are no different, and to whatever degree you can, you want to provide the security and supports so that they know your door is open and want to have lunch with the right other board members, who have your best interest and the students' best interests at heart.

Superintendent as Lead Learner is one who, through example, models an annual willingness (summer retreat or otherwise) to step away from one's comfort zone and learn something new that might benefit one's leadership, the group's governance, or the district's ability to learn and educate. This Lead Learner not only amasses increasing knowledge regarding the technical aspects of instructional leadership, but also focuses on people management. Through their reading, research, and willingness to step outside their comfort zones, hero makers demonstrate their ability to recognize when they must begin to do things differently and make changes in things that are difficult for them. The best learning happens at the edge of uncomfortability (Donlan & Gruenert, 2016).

In order for board members to be comfortable with discomfort, they must witness vicariously the fact that you are benefiting from it, and that you are reflecting on the good it has done you.

Yet in order for board members to be comfortable with discomfort, they must witness vicariously the fact that you are benefiting from it, and that you are reflecting on the good it has done you. Think of it this way: When board members are resistant to the changes you are making (because they are uncomfortable with them), you want them to understand that this may be a sign that they have an opportunity to grow and enjoy the learning as a result. You can't expect them to think and analyze this; they must see it and feel it, to become true believers. This is what your modeling as Lead Learner will allow.

Superintendent as Vision Gatherer is one who can reach deeply and authentically into the minds and hearts of those assembled on the board to hear what is important to them, to validate what they bring in terms of passion and perspective, and to gather these sometimes disparate belief systems into a context where productive discussion can take place. Key to this role is a hero maker's ability to put things into context, simply and clearly. One of the most important skills of a true executive is the ability to take ideas that are incredibly complex and simplify them in a way that brings people together with a concrete understanding of what is going on and in a way that they can simply and quickly relay to others why they are on board with your vision. One particularly important tool here is your ability to use metaphor that is in line with each board member's interests, aptitudes,

One of the most important skills of a true executive is the ability to take ideas that are incredibly complex and simplify them in a way that brings people together.

and abilities. One vision may take seven or eight metaphors to explain—a general metaphor for the group and an individual one for each board member.

Superintendent as Consensus-Builder is one who can begin the hard work of helping board members analyze, synthesize, and prioritize their visions for the school district into a smart, workable policy and budgetary allocation plan for the year in a manner in which all "can live with that." This does not involve taking votes, or even making a decision based on advisory input; it involves complex creation of a plan such as a strategic plan where the product is greater than the sum of its parts, and all involved can see the value, especially in terms of what they may be forgoing individually to experience the biggest win on behalf of schools, children, and community. Key to this role is a hero maker's ability to allow everyone to have a voice, and allow everyone to have enough time with their voices so that they are satisfied that they have been heard. Donlan and Gruenert (2016) note a strategy where facilitators use the power of the circle, a technique gleaned and adapted from the teachings of noted conflict resolution and consensus-building specialist Bob Chadwick from Consensus Associates. What this would entail is the superintendent or board president, during a strategic planning session, asking each board member to share his or her perspective and/or to "pass" when moving from one person to the next. Each person would share uninterrupted and without debate. Important here is for the facilitator to move around the boardroom table a second time, so that those who are more introverted (or those who may have "passed") can have the time to reflect and offer something that may be incredibly substantive the next time around. Techniques such as these forge onsensus, and thus buy-in to what hero makers are trying to advance.

Superintendent as Quality-Assurance Provider is one who can be relied on to keep a close and careful look over the resources being allocated by the board to conduct the community's educational business. It involves delegating, smartly, but only to those persons who have the willingness and capability to exercise extreme talent on behalf of the public's trust and resources. Quality-Assurance Providing also involves anticipating problems before they surface rather than playing Whack-a-Mole with things that are not anticipated. It involves keeping the board president in the loop and seeking out his or her perspective on a weekly basis with great trust and candor. It also involves at times pulling triggers on ideas and even terminating those employees who let the district down. All of the current cries in education for instructional leadership are nice; however, if the business of schools is not being run effectively—if the money and resources are not ample to provide what is needed for leaders to lead, teachers to teach, and learners to learn, then no amount of curricular leadership is going to keep a superintendent in a position to wield influence as a hero maker.

> **If the business of schools is not being run effectively . . . then no amount of curricular leadership is going to keep a superintendent in a position to wield influence as a hero maker.**

Superintendent as Steward means serving through any given year as one who is trusted, and is approachable regarding all facets of school district operation, even with respect to the leadership the superintendent is providing. Stewarding involves much more listening than talking, with a careful balance of deliberating and acting. It also involves parenting and doing what parents do in the care and upbringing of those who depend on them. It does not always involve giving people what they want, yet rather, providing what people need to grow, develop, succeed, and eventually actualize. A wise steward is his or her toughest critic and models this for others to follow. A steward is one who cares, intrinsically, for the good of the whole, as well as the good of all the parts that make up the whole. The best stewards know that "it is people, not programs," that make a difference; they recognize the "I" in team as we noted earlier, and they know that the adults' needs in schools must be attended to first, if we're going to be about children *most*.

Superintendent as Responsibility-Taker accepts full responsibility for *everything* that goes wrong in the entire school district, and gives full credit away for everything that goes right. Key to this role is to embrace personal responsibility for professional realities. This can be an arduous demand on superintendents and something hard to swallow at times, as some school districts are as complicated as small (or large) municipalities, and many things can occur that are outside of superintendents' awareness (marital affairs in the office, embezzlement, and instructional neglect, to name a few). It is really no different than others in similar circumstances—mayors of cities, governors of states, or even the U.S. President. If you are the chief executive, you are where the buck stops. Period. In consideration of such, hero makers find ways to develop organizational acuity so that more things are in their line of vision, as opposed to outside of it. They then feel comfortable in their own skin embracing ambiguity and uncertainty, and dealing with it.

Finally, *Superintendent as Meaning-Maker* finds a way to take an entire year's worth of experience and information, and makes meaning with it in terms of what they report to the board, what the board does with it, and how this affects the continual learning that the board and district experience, so as to have a better next year than last. Key to this role is for hero makers to unearth for the board the value in what they have done in terms of their leadership and governance. This is especially true in what they have done with respect to policy work, as often these efforts do not reap the immediate gratification of the short wins of micromanagement. Thus, it is incredibly important that the hero maker finds ways to allow the board to make meaning of times when it does the right thing—when it stays within the guardrails of its roles and runs the marathon while avoiding the sprints. It involves, as well, teaching board members how to make meaning for their constituencies, so that on reflection, the constituencies will be satisfied with their needs met, and each board member will be seen as a hero for the efforts expended in just and quality leadership.

We really think each of these tasks is possible and all-important for hero makers, as long as satisfied boards of education and communities continue to exist, and further that superintendents know that the basic training for this tour of duty (as well as staying alive in its theatre of operations), requires calisthenics and training in the making of heroes. Calisthenics, one might say, starts with reading this book, or another that is helpful.

Obviously, every leader needs to examine his or her own circumstance, energy, and excitement level. In addition, we all have strengths and weaknesses. Some people find it more fun to mow where the grass is long and others take great satisfaction in keeping a well-manicured lawn. And of course districts change, family needs vary, and board personalities come and go. No one size fits all in terms of alterations, but it sure is more fun to go to work when you are excited to be there and feel that you are making a difference. That is why you chose the job you did, so it also needs to be part of the reason you stay.

No one size fits all in terms of alterations, but it sure is more fun to go to work when you are excited to be there and feel that you are making a difference.

So we ask the same questions here as we did in the beginning of this chapter: Is there a time when it is simply best that superintendents move to another location, so that they can put some more vim and vigor into their leadership? Should hero makers from time to time have a "re-do" on their hero-making?

Our belief is that when a superintendent wanes in either the ability *or interest* of serving "energetically" in the roles described, then an actuary might be tapping on one's shoulder. It might then be time to consider that closing the current door of district-level service might open another window of opportunity, for both the superintendent and the community.

★ Hero-making Tips

◆ Hero makers are honest when they look in the mirror and reflect on their actuarial table. They don't crane their neck or put on too much hair color. They make an honest appraisal of their "dog years" and are not hesitant to ask someone they trust who is candid with feedback.

◆ Hero makers recognize if their desire is to be career-bound, or place-bound. This is important because one's bound-ness has implications for leadership and decisions. Unchecked, this can lead to bias in decision making, so hero makers ask a trusted number-two to keep close watch on their blind spots.

◆ Hero makers teach their boards that as superintendents might have actuarial tables, boards of education possibly do as well. Sometimes the length of a board member's service can adversely impact one's perspective, if one becomes disenchanted with the challenges faced or disinterested in topics that reach the board's attention time and again. This is best discussed in good times, not in bad.

◆ Hero makers, when they exit for new pursuits, leave the schools and the board of education in better places than they found them upon arrival.

Reference

Donlan, R., & Gruenert, S. (2016). *Minds Unleashed: How Principals Can Lead the Right-Brained Way*. Lanham, MD: Rowman & Littlefield Education.

Epilogue: What Next? Toward "Difference-making"

So, you are probably getting pretty good, or you were already very good, at hero-making. We are glad to offer what we can so that you can have outstanding relationships with your board, or at minimum, professional ones, as you [*insert important words*] on behalf of the children in your schools.

What are these important words?

"Make a difference," of course.

You see, as you close this book, something else will happen around you. If you look closely enough, you will see opening up a window of opportunity.

It's a whole new day!

You now have the opportunity to make a difference, not just *for* your board members, principals, teachers, students, families, and communities, but rather *through* your board members, principals, teachers, students, families, and communities.

Hero-making allows for difference-making *through* other people, and here is why.

We have already shared that board members can become hero makers, too. In fact, this is one of your greatest teachable moments: Showing them how. Once doing that, the investment reaps dividends as those who know and communicate with board members feel like heroes, in turn the board members are getting their own needs met (as they are heroes), and when everyone is feeling pretty good, it is much easier to put the collective brainpower into problem solving, planning, and even preventing issues from coming our way.

It is like a performance-enhancing supplement for ensuring everyone brings their A-game to the relationships you have and to the important work you are trying to get accomplished.

u all have a better ability to make a difference, once board
ᵉrs are hero-made, than before they wore that title.

The Difference Maker

Consider this: Your core incentive to becoming a teacher was to make a difference. Then you became a school-level leader to have even more of an impact. Eventually, you became a district-level leader to have even more of a positive influence on students. Even if you did not take the specific path just described, you have arrived at the same point. You do not want simply to make time pass or get through another school year.

You want to make a difference. That is what is at the core of each of our educator's souls.

We are not just in education for the money and glory (that was supposed to be funny, by the way). We have chosen to be educators to affect generations, way beyond our own. We aim to leave a legacy that lasts far beyond our working years. So does almost everyone else who is in our profession. What we must do is to help align being a hero with doing the right thing. By choosing the correct path, we will feel and be more valued than if we choose a *look-at-me* or less-important road. Once people internalize these connections, they then have the ability to focus solely on making a difference.

Not for them, but for others.

That is why we chose education.

That is why we choose to lead.

Just as we teach others how to become heroes, we also have to provide the path for others to be difference-makers. At the end of the day, we know we are in the right profession when we look in the mirror and see that tired face and realize what we do really matters.

We want to make a difference. We want to have a positive impact for years to come.

Just as we teach others how to become heroes, we also have to provide the path for others to be difference-makers. At the end of the day, we know we are in the right profession when we look in the mirror and see that tired face and realize what we do really matters.

It reminds us of the story leaders share when they say they only hire people better than themselves.

Lots of people say it.

Few people do it.

Most are too threatened really to seek out talent. Ironically, rather than hiring people better than ourselves in a holistic way, we typically are seeking those who are more talented or knowledgeable than we are in a specific area. It may be technology, curriculum, or special education. Whatever it is, if leaders consistently hire truly outstanding people, they have not hired anyone more talented than they are.

Because selecting and attracting excellence may be the best talent there is.

We also must reflect on the fact that every time we arrange for someone to be a hero, we become more of one ourselves. Inviting other people to feel like a hero allows them see you as one.

Perhaps that is our greatest gift. Making heroes. Making a difference.

Thanks for doing both. Our students deserve it.

Special Feature: Board Personalities and the Process Communication Model® (PCM)

The *way something is said* is more important than *what is said*, because of the needs we have in communication and the personalities we have within us (Collignon, Legrand, & Parr, 2010; Kahler, 2008). Hero makers understand and apply this to their interactions with board members.

Each of us has a unique personality structure made up of six personality energies (or personality types). Our base personality is strongest and is developed at birth or shortly thereafter, with the remaining five personalities layering in to form a more comprehensive personality composition, typically prior to age seven (Kahler, 2008). We all have each of the six personality types (personality energies), and these personalities can arrange themselves in one of 720 different ways, from strongest to least strong, within our overall personality structure (Kahler, 2008).

One common attribute of personality that we all have is that each one of us is *all* six of our personalities. We are not just "one type" or another, which we feel is a limitation of the plug-and-play personality typographies used in our profession, many within quick reach on the Internet.

In terms of personality study that can help us with our boards of education, we must keep in mind that as personalities, we are neither a type, color, nor acronym. Each of us (and each of our board members) has a unique and intricate web of personality dynamics—those that we can use to foster better relationships. The talents within those personalities can help board members to be more productive and to govern more effectively.

As superintendents, we can work with our boards to bring out those talents.

PCM teaches us that each of the personalities inside us has different ways of viewing the world (perceptions), different ways of communicating (what we prefer to hear and how we say things), different environmental preferences (how our workspace affects how we work with others), different psychological needs (what we need that gives us the energy to work and live with others positively), and even predictable distress patterns when those psychological needs are not being met (Kahler, 1996, 2015; Kahler, 2008). This is certainly congruent with what we shared in earlier chapters about the needs of individuals and groups, including constituencies.

This understanding is where you as the hero maker can encourage better relationships and increase team performance and cohesiveness.

Learning about the personalities within your board members allows you to provide what those board members need to function well. You will be the person in their lives who "speaks their language."

Learning about the personalities within your board members allows you to provide what those board members need to function well. You will be the person in their lives who "speaks their language"—the hero maker who ensures board members end every conversation with you in a better space than when they began it. PCM is an incredible leadership tool that establishes a positive difference in people's lives through specific skill sets that can be employed for better communication and relationships (Gilbert, 2012; Pauley & Pauley, 2009).

An understanding of PCM might also provide a sense of reassurance to you that when those around you are oppositional or contradictory, it might not be really so much about what you are doing in terms of the technical aspects of your own job performance, as it might be about what is *not* being provided to your board members in their lives. Using a computer metaphor, their own personal hardware, software, and networks are not working well together. You, however, have the opportunity to *be* the technician!

You can do something to affect positively what is occurring.

With PCM, present circumstance is well within your control to influence. You are able to put together a plan of how best to approach your board members so that they can address what is not working well inside them. Here is some information for you to consider regarding PCM, as it will demonstrate how these personality types (or energies) might exist within the typical people with whom you come into contact.

Process Communication Model® (PCM)

The Process Communication Model® (PCM) helps us to understand that communication problems are a mystery only insofar as people are a mystery (Kahler, 2006, 2008). Unpack the layers, take a look at what is going on, and it is pretty straightforward to figure out "What's up?" in situations of miscommunication or poor relationships . . . *and* to determine what to do about it.

Think about those situations where board members are acting, let us say, critical, suspicious, defiant, manipulative, mistake-prone, or timid (Donlan, 2015a). These behaviors are actually a gift, believe it or not (adapted from J. Parr, *The Gift of Drivers*, PCM World Conference, Tokyo, Japan, October, 2013). They are a gift because you as a hero maker can use these symptoms to diagnose what underlying factors are influencing your board members' behavior. You will know how your board members perceive the world and what they need in terms of communication (and how to provide it).

For each of your board members, certain personality energies inside them predominate more than others, and the key is to remember that each board member has *all* of them. It pays to look below the surface. Here are the personality types/energies that comprise all people, and some other important information to consider:

TABLE 14.1 PCM Personality Types, Key Perceptions, and Character Strengths

Personality Types We all have all six of them, layered in terms of their relative strengths.	*Key Perception* The way each personality type views the world initially and consistently.	*Character Strengths* The positive attributes each personality type displays to get things done.
Thinker	Thoughts	Responsible, Logical, and Organized
Persister	Opinions	Dedicated, Conscientious, and Observant
Rebel	Reactions	Spontaneous, Creative, and Playful
Promoter	Actions	Persuasive, Adaptable, and Charming
Harmonizer	Emotions	Compassionate, Sensitive, and Warm
Imaginer	Inactions	Calm, Reflective, and Imaginative

Adapted from Kahler (2008) *The Process Therapy Model: The Six Personality Types with Adaptations*. Little Rock, AR: Taibi Kahler Associates.

As an example, if our board members focus more on data and information, they predominate in **Thinker** personality. Logic is their strength (Kahler, 1996, 2015). When new information is presented at a board meeting, they process the information first through their thoughts. We might often hear them request that options are examined and discussed. On their best days, they would have the ability to "think logically; take in facts and ideas and synthesize them" (Kahler, 1996, 2015, p. 11).

If our board members focus more on loyalty and commitment, they predominate in **Persister** personality. They hold firm to values (Kahler, 1996, 2015). When new information is presented at a board meeting, they first judge whether or not the information is congruent with their beliefs. We might often hear them request how something helps the mission of the school district. On their best days, they have the "ability to give opinions, beliefs, and judgments" (Kahler, 1996, 2015, p. 12).

If our board members resonate more with spontaneity or creativity, they predominate in **Rebel** personality. Humor comes second nature to them (Kahler, 1996, 2015). When new information is presented at a board meeting, they might first react to whether they liked it or not. They can lighten the mood of the room and have an uncanny ability to say aloud what everyone else at the board meeting is thinking silently (Collignon, Legrand, & Parr, 2010). On their best days, they have the "ability to see humor in things and enjoy the present" (Kahler, 1996, 2015, p. 15).

If our board members prize adaptability and self-sufficiency, they predominate in **Promoter** personality. Charm is their strength (Kahler, 1996, 2015). When new information is presented at a board meeting, they look at how it can be implemented right away. We might often hear them say, "Give me the bottom line," or "Enough talk, we need to do something with this." On their best days, they have the "ability to be firm and direct" (Kahler, 1996, 2015, p. 16).

If our board members focus more on family and friendship or how they "feel" for students, they predominate in **Harmonizer** personality. Compassion comes naturally (Kahler, 1996, 2015). When new information is presented at a board meeting, they first filter it through their emotions. We might often hear them say, "Have we considered how people will feel about our decision?" On their best days, they have the "ability to nurture and give to others [as they would be good] as creating harmony" (Kahler, 1996, 2015, p. 13).

If our board members need privacy and their own space, they predominate in **Imaginer** personality. Imagination is their strong suit (Kahler, 1996, 2015). When new information is presented at a board meeting, they do not do anything with it at first. Later in the conversation or when alone, they reflect upon it. We will not often hear them saying much at a board meeting, unless someone suggests they offer comment, or directs them to do so. On their best days, they have the "ability to be introspective [and to work] well with others with things and tasks" (Kahler, 1996, 2015, p. 14).

Again, our board members have all six of these personalities, and they can pull from more than one personality in how they perceive the world. The point here is that hero makers look closely at the favored perceptual frames of their board members through the personality energies noted above, and they use these to connect

Process communication allows hero makers to "speak six languages" second-by-second (the language of personality) simultaneously, and very subtly.

through certain ways of communicating. Process communication allows hero makers to "speak six languages" second-by-second (the language of personality) simultaneously, and very subtly.

PCM provides hero makers with powerful tools to use their own personality energies to put their own selves in a good place, so that they are better able to invite satisfaction and productivity in board members toward better leadership and governance for the school.

Consider the following: In hero-making, a superintendent recognizes first *what can be made*, and *what cannot be made*. For example, it is really a myth to think we can *make* others feel good or bad, or that others can make us feel good or bad (Kahler, 1996, 2015; Kahler, 2008). That is not what hero-making is purporting to do, although admittedly things seem to go better when board members have positive self-concept. PCM gets to the heart of how "hero-making" (our goal) differs from "feeling-making" (a myth).

We must be mindful that any true hero exists [as a hero] in the minds of others, not in one's own mind solely. Sure, we are trying to get board members to understand and appreciate how they can be heroes through their work, and we hope that it is authentic through our success, and with theirs. The challenge lies in its complexity. "Should superintendents be successful in encouraging board member success, heroism may follow . . . but not always. Heroism is perceived by others; we do not bestow it on ourselves" (M. B. Gilbert, personal communication, June 1, 2016).

It is in the context of our working with board members so that they are better able to provide for their own needs that PCM becomes powerful in hero-making, as better interactions influence the probability of our board members' success, and thus increase the chance that others will affirm and validate in board members their hero status.

Hero makers who focus on board member personalities know it is important to recognize what the board members *can* do, as well

as what they might have more difficulty doing. We nc
chapters the importance of our serving as the *shield* f
members, and this will become even clearer here. Wit.
can encourage your board members to play to their stre
your understanding that a mismatch between what is e.,pected of
them and what they have the energy to do is within your control.

Why so?

Each of these personality energies described earlier has underlying psychological needs that, if met, will allow them to access
their best selves, yet if not met, will result in predictable distress
patterns (Kahler, 2008) that may make your leadership very difficult, as you will be dealing with your board members' not-so-
optimal sides. At these times, your board members are wearing
masks, and your relationship with them is more like a primetime
drama. Yet, it does not have to be so. Let us look at each of the six
typical board member psychological needs and corresponding
distress patterns that come about in their absence.

Needs and Distress Patterns

If a board member in Thinker personality is providing for his or
her main psychological need for recognition of work and time
structure, then all is well. Yet, if this need is not being met, the
result can begin a daily or weekly distress sequence of being per-
fectionistic and being unwilling to delegate, taking on too much
(Kahler, 1996, 2015; Kahler, 2008). Thinker personality in further
distress can even become frustrated and angry with others, and
may even verbally attack. It sounds like, "Can't people get here on
time?!" and "That was a stupid thing to say!" (Kahler, 1996, 2015;
Kahler, 2008). Hero makers provide for recognition of work and
time structure for those in Thinker personality and minimize the
chance that this sequence of distress will become a part of board
governance. Doing so may reduce micromanagement by board
members.

If a board member in Persister personality is providing for his
or her main psychological need for recognition of work and convictions, then all is well, yet if this need is not being met, the result

can begin a daily or weekly distress sequence of focusing on things that are wrong, rather than on those things that are right (Kahler, 1996, 2015; Kahler, 2008). Persister personality in further distress can even become hyperconvictional, pushing beliefs with righteous anger. It sounds like, "You should . . . !" and "I can't believe that you . . . !" (Kahler, 1996, 2015; Kahler, 2008). Hero makers provide for recognition of work and convictions for those in Persister personality and minimize the chance that this sequence of distress will become a part of board governance. Doing so may reduce unwanted grandstanding of board members in public.

If a board member in Rebel personality is providing for his or her main psychological need for playful contact, then all is well, yet if this need is not being met, the result can begin a daily or weekly distress sequence of reacting quickly and disliking something before fully understanding it, or behaving if something is too hard to understand (Kahler, 1996, 2015; Kahler, 2008). Rebel personality in further distress will blame others. It sounds like, "This sucks!" "I don't get it; this is awful!" and "Yes, but it's not my fault!" (Kahler, 1996, 2015; Kahler, 2008). Hero makers provide for playful contact for those in Rebel personality and minimize the chance that this sequence of distress will become a part of board governance. Doing so may reduce negative reactions in board members that occur on the spot.

If a board member in Promoter personality is providing for his or her main psychological need for incidence (lots of action, quickly), then all is well, yet if this need is not being met, the result can begin a daily or weekly distress sequence of expecting others to fend for themselves (Kahler, 1996, 2015; Kahler, 2008). Promoter personality in further distress can even start to manipulate people or instigate a "Let's you and him fight." It sounds like, "Can't take it, huh?" "Sometimes you just gotta suck it up and do your job." "Did you hear what he said about you? Are you going to take that?" (Kahler, 1996, 2015; Kahler, 2008). Hero makers provide for incidence for those in Promoter personality and minimize the chance that this sequence of distress will become a part of board governance. It may reduce the whispers by a board member that lead to vote swinging against you.

If a board member in Harmonizer personality is providing for his or her main psychological need for recognition of person and sensory needs, then all is well, yet if this need is not being met, the result can begin a daily or weekly distress sequence of becoming wishy-washy in decision making and being overly concerned with everyone's feelings and overadapting to them (Kahler, 1996, 2015; Kahler, 2008). Harmonizer personality in further distress makes mistakes that are atypical, and even invites others to criticize them (self-denigration). It sounds like, "Do you think maybe we could possibly . . . ?" "Oh, I'm just so stupid." "I know that it'll all just go south next week." (Kahler, 1996, 2015; Kahler, 2008). Hero makers provide the psychological need for recognition of person and sensory needs for those in Harmonizer personality and minimize the chance that this sequence of distress will become a part of board governance. It may reduce board members' overadapting after public comment.

If a board member in Imaginer personality is providing for his or her main psychological need for solitude, then all is well; if this need is not being met, the result can begin a daily or weekly distress sequence of withdrawing and putting up shields to communication (Kahler, 1996, 2015; Kahler, 2008). Imaginer personality in further distress can even withdraw more fully, possibly not showing up at your board meetings. It often sounds like silence or one giving the impression that others are in charge of this person's behavior, "I wasn't given the authority to . . ." (Kahler, 1996, 2015; Kahler, 2008). Hero makers provide for solitude for those in Imaginer personality and minimize the chance that this sequence of distress will become a part of board governance. It may help improve your chances of a board quorum (because those in Imaginer will take part) and of reflective decision making.

Dr. Nate Regier, Co-Founding Owner, and his team at Next Element remind us, "Drama [is] good for ratings; bad for business." We don't want drama with our boards. PCM Master Trainer Dr. Michael Gilbert notes how PCM can help us listen carefully to what is being said and "how," in order to resolve conflicts when they occur in K-12 leadership (Gilbert, 2012).

So what is a hero maker to do?

Board Personalities: Hero-making and PCM

An increasing awareness that school board members are very much like the students enrolled in our schools is helpful in determining the utility of PCM for practicing superintendents. In reflecting upon the Process Communication Model's usefulness, Gilbert (1994) described that the model as so precise that one can anticipate another's actual distress behaviors before they are even exhibited, with the use of this information allowing one knowledgeable to intervene before miscommunication and distress even begins.

Hero makers can do this with their boards as well.

It merits mentioning again that hero makers are not enamored by quick, online personality inventories that paint personality as this or that "type." They know that any model that is a snapshot of one's personality is just that: a snapshot.

Where PCM is different is that it is more like a video motion picture of one's life: illustrating where someone's personality was at birth, how it grew and developed to the present day, and where it might move over an entire lifetime. That is useful information!

Yet, please be encouraged to make your own decisions on whether the information we are sharing is applicable to you. You are your best judge. Our intent is simply to share the best information that we have found that is worth your time.

With that in mind, our opinion is that no matter what you are doing in a school district in terms of school improvement of people or programs, PCM will serve as a shot-in-the-arm, or a catalyst, to better ensure that what you are doing is even more powerful and sustainable (Donlan, 2013). As we dispelled the more common adage in earlier chapters, PCM acknowledges and respects each "I" in team and shows what is happening beneath the surface of everyone you work with, and of course yourself. Teachers can use it in the classroom with their students; principals with their teachers. You can use it with your principals and board members, even with those in your community.

What about when board members and others become more challenging—when they are in distress? This is a hero maker's opportunity to connect with them and invite them out of a place of discomfort.

We noted above what the typical distressed behavior looks like in each of the personalities we all have. The chart on the next page is helpful in putting this all together at a glance.

What is a hero maker to do?

A deeper dive into PCM (more than this book would have time for) would allow for a second-by-second and minute-by-minute "how-to," yet for the purpose of our discussion here, some important items can be noted that will help you immediately when encountering personality distress in your board (defined as board members not getting their needs met positively).

First of all, in terms of the desire of all on your board to be perceived as heroes, each board member is actually asking a subconscious question of himself or herself. The question varies depending on the personalities within them that have the strongest motivational influence. Knowing what these questions are can help hero makers more effectively coach their boards. Examples are as follows:

When board members are motivated most in their Thinker personality, a subconscious question having to do with their desire to be a hero asks, "Am I competent?" (Collignon, Legrand, & Parr, 2010; Kahler, 2008). If these board members consider themselves competent and think those who embrace them as heroes do so as well, then they will more often see themselves as worthwhile (and others, too), minimizing the potential for distress (Kahler, 2008). Hero makers at board meetings can facilitate this by supplying these board members with relevant information, offering options, and letting them decide for themselves on items of discussion (Collignon, Legrand, & Parr, 2010; Donlan 2015a; Donlan 2015b; Kahler, 2008).

When board members are motivated most in their Persister personality, a subconscious question having to do with their desire to be a hero asks, "Am I trustworthy?" (Collignon, Legrand, & Parr, 2010; Kahler, 2008). If these board members consider themselves trustworthy to those who depend on them and if they believe those who embrace them as heroes do so as well, then they will more often see themselves as worthwhile (and others, too),

TABLE 14.2 PCM Psychological Needs and Distress Patterns

Personalities within Us	Psychological Needs	Daily or Weekly Distress	Further into Distress	What This Sounds Like
Thinker	Recognition of Work and Time Structure	Perfectionistic, Unwillingness to Delegate, and Taking on Too Much	Frustrated and Angry with Others, May Verbally Attack	"Can't people get here on time?" and "That was a stupid thing to say!"
Persister	Recognition of Work and Convictions	Focus on Things that Are Wrong, Rather than What is Right	Hyperconvictional; Pushing Beliefs with Righteous Anger; Grandstanding	"You should ...!" and "I can't believe that you ...!"
Rebel	Playful Contact	React Quickly/ Disliking Something before Understanding It Fully	Blaming Others; Wanting Others to Take Responsibility for Them	"This sucks!" "I hate this." "I don't get it; this is awful!" "Yes, but it's not my fault!"
Promoter	Incidence	Expects Others to Fend for Themselves	Provokes Negative Excitement and Drama; Further Manipulates	"Can't take it, huh?" "Sometimes you just gotta suck it up and do your job." "Did you hear what he said about you?" "Are you going to take that?"
Harmonizer	Recognition of Person and Sensory	Becoming Wishy-Washy in Decision Making; Overly Concerned with Everyone's Feelings	Makes Mistakes that Are Atypical; Invites Others to Criticize Them (self-denigrating)	"Do you think maybe we could possibly ...?" "Oh, I'm just so stupid" "I know that it'll all just go south next week."
Imaginer	Solitude	Withdraw; Put Up Shields to Communication	Withdraw Even More Fully; Question Their Own Adequacy and Initiative	[Silence] "I wasn't given the authority to ..."

Adapted from Kahler (2008) *The Process Therapy Model: The Six Personality Types with Adaptations.* Little Rock, AR: Taibi Kahler Associates.

minimizing the potential for distress (Kahler, 2008). Hero makers at board meetings can facilitate this by listening attentively to what these board members say, noting the positives in their beliefs, pointing out areas of agreement, and repeating what they say to show that they are listening to their opinions (Collignon, Legrand, & Parr, 2010; Donlan 2015a; Donlan 2015b; Kahler, 2008).

When board members are motivated most in their Rebel personality, a subconscious question having to do with their desire to be a hero asks, "Am I acceptable as I am?" (Collignon, Legrand, & Parr, 2010; Kahler, 2008). If these board members consider themselves acceptable *as they are,* and if they are acceptable as they are to those who embrace them as heroes, then they will more often see themselves as worthwhile (and others, too), minimizing the potential for distress (Kahler, 2008). Hero makers at board meetings can facilitate this by having a relaxed attitude to these board members' reactions, mirroring their nonverbals, reflecting their expressions, using humor, and accepting their distaste for formal protocol or convention (Collignon, Legrand, & Parr, 2010; Donlan 2015a; Donlan 2015b; Kahler, 2008).

When board members are motivated most in their Promoter personality, a subconscious question having to do with their desire to be a hero asks, "Am I alive?" (Collignon, Legrand, & Parr, 2010; Kahler, 2008). If these board members consider themselves alive through their efforts as a hero, and if others see them as a hero that is relevant and alive in the moment ("bringing home the big one"), then they will more often see themselves as worthwhile (and others, too), minimizing the potential for distress (Kahler, 2008). Hero makers at board meetings can facilitate this by recognizing their achievements publicly, accepting these board members' needs to tell about their own accomplishments (not thinking of it as bragging or boasting), and accepting their dislike for order and procedures (Collignon, Legrand, & Parr, 2010; Donlan 2015a; Donlan 2015b; Kahler, 2008).

When board members are motivated most in their Harmonizer personality, a subconscious question having to do with their desire to be a hero asks, "Am I loveable?" (Collignon, Legrand, & Parr, 2010; Kahler, 2008). If these board members consider themselves loveable to those closest to them and believe those who embrace them as heroes love them as well, they will more often see themselves as worthwhile (and others too), minimizing the potential for distress (Kahler, 2008). Hero makers at board meetings can facilitate this by showing an understanding of these board members' feelings and offering them encouragement (Collignon, Legrand, & Parr, 2010; Donlan 2015a; Donlan 2015b; Kahler, 2008).

When board members are motivated most in their Imaginer personality, a subconscious question having to do with their desire to be a hero asks, "Am I wanted?" (Collignon, Legrand, & Parr, 2010; Kahler, 2008). If these board members consider themselves wanted by those who embrace them as heroes, they will more often see themselves as worthwhile (and others, too), minimizing the potential for distress (Kahler, 2008). Hero makers at board meetings can facilitate this by accepting that these board members need time alone, knowing that in their silence may be some deep reflection about the issues under discussion, providing them the space to reflect, and using brief, direct exchanges with them (Collignon, Legrand, & Parr, 2010; Donlan 2015a; Donlan 2015b; Kahler, 2008).

We find that among the discoveries we have made in hero-making, Dr. Taibi Kahler's discoveries in PCM serve as an excellent catalyst for what we are suggesting you do. The comprehensive nature of PCM could span an entire book or more, so we will stop here for now. What we *can* do for you directly in the rest of this chapter is to offer a few typical challenging board member examples (archetypes), and what may be going on in their personalities, so that you can get a better idea of how to connect with PCM in hero-making.

Challenging Board Member Examples

What is profound in the information provided by the PCM model is that in some cases, your board members are predominantly motivated in different personalities at different times based on the issues that present themselves in their lives and how they respond to them (Kahler, 2008). As changes in personality energy take time, you would see this more in the case of a board member who serves for many years, or one who served years ago and has returned. Most often, the board member who is elected stays motived predominantly in the same personality among those described in this Special Feature. More intriguing, in two-thirds of your board members, the personalities in which they communicate most naturally may be different than those through which they are motivated (Kahler, 1996, 2015; Kahler, 2008). Imagine knowing that!

Where this is particularly relevant to hero makers is that what people appear to be on the outside might not actually be what they are on the inside. Our best hero makers will unearth these discoveries, in order to connect and make a difference. Consider a few challenging board member archetypes here and the possibilities of what might be going on in their personalities. The key here is that we must look beyond the immediate surface behavior to plan a best approach in dealing with the behavior, because the same behaviors can have different personality influences.

> We must look beyond the immediate surface behavior to plan a best approach in dealing with the behavior, because the same behaviors can have different personality influences.

The Rogue: Many of us have board members who, no matter what is decided in board meetings, are running amok with their own agendas, doing their own things, and not seeming to care for the consequences. These board members might be in Rebel personality distress. If so, they are inviting some negative contact with those around them, while in actuality, starving for positive or playful contact. But then again, if there is an underlying agenda that is a bit more consistent, they may have some pretty strong Persister personality distress as well with a need to have their beliefs affirmed. They may be staunchly hyper-convictional on behalf of an important constituency. And if you or the board is going in a direction that contradicts their constituencies (to them, they want to be a hero), all the logic in the world might not appeal to them. You might also find that these board members are in Promoter personality distress with a need for incidence (some risk needed, with the potential for a payoff). This might be the cause of the Rogue behavior.

The key here is to watch what is going on, and then try to ascertain *why*. You can then focus on the board members' psychological needs when beginning the conversation.

That is what hero-making is all about; meeting Rogues where they are, nonjudgmentally. That is what PCM allows us to do: find a way to meet people where they are in terms of their psychological needs being met. Address the need by saying or doing something that satisfies the need's hunger. Then communicate in a way that best resonates. Seek to understand, so that you can validate and work from there. At minimum, you will understand what these board members need in order to return to productivity and sound leadership. You may actually find a way that these board members can align with what you want to do or align with the rest of the board.

The Bean Counter: No matter the locale, it seems that there is typically someone on the board who is more about numbers than people. Every line needs a number, and every line item must reconcile, and everything must be in its place, sort of like the parallel nature of the horizontal lines on the Bean Counter's forehead.

The first thing to remember about this personality structure, often predominating in Thinker, is the Bean Counter's need to be *asked* about options, as there is general distress among Bean Counters when being *told* what the options are. Bean Counters while beginning their Thinker personality distress sequences have the need to appear perfectly capable to others—smart, as well—and will often over-detail or use qualifying statements to get their perspectives (like "perfectly capable"), uttered "just right." It would sound like, "*In reviewing the budgetary allocations—and I say this in due deference to the board president's authority to do this on her own—I have found some items that may be prudent to consider for a reduction in expenses.*" Not in distress, the Bean Counter might say instead, "*I think it is important that we discuss a few items that can save costs.*"

Picking up on these things will be your key to affirming a Bean Counter's Thinker personality need for recognition of work, and also awareness that things must happen on time. Bean Counters in Thinker personality are often less apt to jump into a conversation dominated by others, so your taking time to recognize them during the discussion and mentioning to others that you would like to ask their thoughts so that the options can be fully vetted, will go a long way. From time to time, Bean Counters in Thinker distress will get frustrated and angry about things that appear to be stupid or illogical to them and can bring a real bite to any boardroom table. You can do something about that.

The Bully: Keeping in mind those *factors of circumstance* presented earlier in the book, this board member, like most bullies in the schoolyard, was probably bullied prior and is taking it out on you or on others at this point. Factors of circumstance are probably much more in play than factors of personality. This person might be getting bullied by a spouse, a boss at work, or even his or her own children.

It is important to separate bullying (calculated, repeated behavior over time) from distressed behavior that has to do with personality and a lack of needs fulfillment (Kahler, 2008). One example from a personality standpoint has to do with one's Promoter personality, with a specific perspective brought about while in distress, such as when those in Promoter personality have the perspective, "Can't take it, huh?" This is not really bullying. It has more to do with what those in Promoter personality are not getting in terms of communication and needs fulfillment, than it does with one acting on a power imbalance with another intentionally. Recognizing the factors of distress noted in this chapter will help separate genuine Promoter distress (lack of needs fulfillment of "incidence") from bullying, and the situations must be handled differently.

Hero makers recognize that if board members are in a Promoter personality distress pattern, the need for incidence (again, a bit of risk or excitement) is of paramount importance. Give them something to do, to "bring home" with some action or risk and where they will be celebrated publicly, while saying, *"Look, I'll make you a deal. Tell me what you need to pull in the reins here, and there will be something in it for you."* This will validate their own potency and work to meet their needs.

Aside from Promoter personality distress, bullying is another issue. With bullies, like the definitions in our schools, it is a pattern of behavior with a power imbalance. Note that because of other circumstances in that person's life, a bully probably cycles at times from being a Persecutor, to being a Victim, and even a Rescuer, with drama ever-present. The dance of drama may actually be more natural for this person than a compassionate alternative, as that is what someone in a drama dance knows, and where he or she feels more comfortable (Regier & King, 2013).

It is odd, but true. And sad.

Bullies may need more direct intervention with the help of the board president (with support and guidance by the hero maker, of course), if they do not get themselves under control.

*****

Other challenging personalities that are equally complicated exist in many of our schools, including Joe Six Pack, The Backstabber, The Climber, the Yes-Man/Woman, The Clueless Advocate, and many others. Hero makers unpack the layers of personality, figuring out how these board members are looking at things and what they need in terms of their communication and their psychological needs.

Hero makers unpack the layers of personality, figuring out how these board members are looking at things and what they need in terms of their communication and their psychological needs.

Hero makers find that PCM allows them to have positive and lasting impact.

As we have tried to demonstrate in our book, focusing on the "*I*" in team is critical. Personal identity through personality is foundationally important to each and every board member, even if they will not admit it or cannot. Hero makers intentionally position the "*I*'s" in a team to work together toward the benefit of all. It is especially important that through a focus on the needs of the adults in our schools, the success of children is paramount, as children are your greatest responsibility and are hopefully going to consider your board members heroes.

⊛ Hero-making Tips

◆ Hero makers actively search for theory, inside and outside of the field of educational leadership, that allows them to bring out the hero in others. They resist the temptation to embrace the war stories of those who have gone before them as the only way to handle challenges, yet they do not discount them either.

◆ Hero makers do not put people in boxes when thinking about personality. They do not rely on quick fixes, trendy typologies, or broad brushstrokes when working to understand their boards or themselves. They understand that board members are *in* one of their six personalities at any given moment; they are not simply *a* single personality.

◆ Hero makers first ask themselves, "Are my psychological needs being met?" Because if they are not, the hero maker will be unable to address effectively someone else in distress.

◆ Hero makers understand that board members may *hear* with one part of their personality (typically the strongest in terms of communication), yet may make decisions with either that part, or another part (typically the strongest in motivation).

(Collignon, Legrand, & Parr, 2010; Kahler, 2008)

◆ Hero makers realize that distressed board member behavior is really a "mask," hiding the real person inside. They will forgive in advance and then take active steps to provide intervention to address that person's psychological need.

(Kahler, 2008)

◆ Hero makers realize that as distress in some invites distress in others, the potential exists for superintendents to respond to negative board behavior with a mask of distress, if they themselves are not providing for their own needs prior to each board meeting or interaction.

(Kahler, 2008)

Coauthor Dr. Ryan Donlan is a Master Trainer in the Process Communication Model® (PCM) and the Process Education Model® (PEM) [*with appreciation to Michael Gilbert, Joe and Judy Pauley, and Taibi Kahler*].

Thanks to Dr. Taibi Kahler for his intellectual leadership and the creation and evolution of the Process Communication Model® (PCM) and kind review of this feature for intellectual accuracy.

Thanks to Gerard Collignon and Kahler Communications Incorporated (KCI) for permission to present select PCM concepts and applications in *The Hero Maker*.

Thanks to Dr. Michael Gilbert for his permissions and edits, and continued friendship and guidance. Michael of ATOIRE Communication owns the North American rights to educational applications of PCM, The Process Education Model® (PEM) and is a PCM/PEM Master Trainer.

Thanks to Cyril Collignon, PCM Master Trainer, and Gerard Collignon, PCM Certifying Master Trainer, global leaders of KCI, for their friendship and support in sharing PCM scholarship, application, and writing to leaders everywhere.

References

Collignon, G., Legrand, P., & Parr, J. (2010). *Parlez-vous Personality: Process Communication for Coaches*. Paris, France: InterEditions-Dunod.

Donlan, R. (2013). The Process Education Model (PEM): A Catalyst for School Improvement. *Journal of Process Communication, 1* (1), 45–67.

Donlan, R. (2015a, January). The Power of Process in Board Meetings. *AASA New Superintendent's E-Journal*. Alexandria, VA: American Association of School Administrators.

Donlan, R. (2015b, April). Speaking the Language of Board Meetings. *School Administrator*. Alexandria, VA: American Association of School Administrators.

Gilbert, M. B. (1994). Meeting Communication Needs of Students Can Promote Success: An Excerpt of an Off-Campus Duty Assignment. University of Arkansas at Little Rock.

Gilbert, M. B. (2012). *Communicating Effectively: Tools for Educational Leaders*. (2nd ed.). Lanham, MD: Rowman & Littlefield Education.

Kahler, T. (1996, 2015). *The Process Communication Model® Seminar: Seminar One/Core Topics*. Hot Springs, AR: Kahler Communications, Inc.

Kahler, T. (2006). *The Mastery of Management: Or How to Solve the Mystery of Mismanagement*. Little Rock, AR: Taibi Kahler Associates, Inc.

Kahler, T. (2008). *The Process Therapy Model: The Six Personality Types with Adaptations*. Little Rock, AR: Taibi Kahler Associates, Inc.

Pauley, J., & Pauley, J. (2009). *Communication: The Key to Effective Leadership*. Milwaukee, WI: American Society for Quality.

Regier, N., & King, J. (2013). *Beyond Drama: Transcending Energy Vampires*. Newton, KS: Next Element Publishing.